Animal
Farm

by George Orwell

Kevin Radford

Series Editors:
Sue Bennett and Dave Stockwin

HODDER
EDUCATION
AN HACHETTE UK COMPANY

The Publishers would like to thank the following for permission to reproduce copyright material.

Photo credits

p. 8 AF archive/Alamy; **p. 10** TopFoto; **p. 13** Ingram; **p. 17** Photos 12/Alamy; **p. 19** AF archive/Alamy; **p. 24** TopFoto; **p. 40** AF archive/Alamy; **p. 45** Photos 12/Alamy

Every effort has been made to trace all copyright holders, but if any have been inadvertently overlooked, the Publishers will be pleased to make the necessary arrangements at the first opportunity.

Although every effort has been made to ensure that website addresses are correct at time of going to press, Hodder Education cannot be held responsible for the content of any website mentioned in this book. It is sometimes possible to find a relocated web page by typing in the address of the home page for a website in the URL window of your browser.

Hachette UK's policy is to use papers that are natural, renewable and recyclable products and made from wood grown in sustainable forests. The logging and manufacturing processes are expected to conform to the environmental regulations of the country of origin.

Orders: please contact Bookpoint Ltd, 130 Park Drive, Milton Park, Abingdon, Oxon OX14 4SE. Telephone: (44) 01235 827720. Fax: (44) 01235 400454. Email education@bookpoint.co.uk Lines are open from 9 a.m. to 5 p.m., Monday to Saturday, with a 24-hour message answering service. You can also order through our website: www.hoddereducation.co.uk

ISBN: 978 1 4718 5354 8

© Kevin Radford, 2016

First published in 2016 by

Hodder Education,

An Hachette UK Company

Carmelite House

50 Victoria Embankment

London EC4Y 0DZ

www.hoddereducation.co.uk

Impression number	10 9 8 7 6 5 4 3 2 1
Year	2020 2019 2018 2017 2016

Cover photo © THEPALMER/Getty Images

Illustrations by Integra Software Services Pvt. Ltd.

Typeset in Bliss light 11/13pt by Integra Software Services Pvt. Ltd., Pondicherry, India

Printed in Italy

A catalogue record for this title is available from the British Library.

Contents

Getting the most from this guide

This guide is designed to help you to raise your achievement in your examination response to *Animal Farm*. It is intended for you to use throughout your GCSE English literature course. It will help you when you are studying the novel for the first time and also during your revision.

The following features have been used throughout this guide to help you focus your understanding of the novel.

Target your thinking

A list of **introductory questions** labelled by Assessment Objective is provided at the beginning of each chapter to give you a breakdown of the material covered. They target your thinking in order to help you work more efficiently by focusing on the key messages.

Build critical skills

These boxes offer an opportunity to consider some **more challenging questions**. They are designed to encourage deeper thinking, analysis and exploratory thought. Building and practising critical skills in this way will give you a real advantage in the examination.

GRADE *FOCUS*

It is possible to know a novel well and yet still underachieve in the examination if you are unsure what the examiners are looking for. The **GRADE FOCUS** boxes give a clear explanation of how you may be assessed, with an emphasis on the criteria for gaining a Grade 5 and a Grade 8.

REVIEW YOUR LEARNING

At the end of each chapter you will find this section to **test your knowledge**: a series of short, specific questions to ensure you have understood and absorbed the key messages of the chapter. Answers to the 'Review your learning' questions are provided in the final section of the guide (p. 102).

GRADE *BOOSTER*

Read and remember these pieces of helpful **grade-boosting advice**. They provide top tips from experienced teachers and examiners who can advise you on what to do, as well as what *not* to do, in order to maximise your chances of success in the examination.

Key quotation

Key quotations are highlighted for you, so that if you wish you may use them as **supporting evidence** in your examination answers. Further quotations, grouped by characterisation, top moments and themes, can be found in the 'Top ten' section on page 96 of the guide.

'Yes it was theirs – everything that they could see was theirs!'

Studying the text

You may find it useful to dip into this guide in sections as and when you need them, rather than reading it from start to finish. For example, the section on 'Context' can be read before you read the novel itself, since it offers an explanation of the relevant historical, cultural and literary background to the text. In 'Context' you will find information about aspects of George Orwell's life and times that influenced his writing; the particular issues with which Orwell was concerned; and where the novel stands in terms of the literary tradition to which it belongs.

The 'Plot and structure' sections in this guide could be helpful to you either before or after you read each chapter of *Animal Farm*. As well as a summary of events there is also commentary, so that you are aware of both the key events and the literary features in each chapter. Later, the sections on 'Characterisation', 'Themes' and 'Language, style and analysis' will help develop your thinking further, in preparation for written responses on particular aspects of the text.

Many students also enjoy the experience of being able to bring something extra to their classroom lessons in order to be a step ahead of the game. Alternatively, you may have missed a classroom session or feel that you need a clearer explanation, and the guide can help you with this too.

An initial reading of the section on 'Assessment Objectives and skills' will enable you to make really effective notes in preparation for assessments, because you will have a very clear understanding of what the examiners are looking for. The Assessment Objectives are what examination boards base their mark schemes on. In this section the AOs are broken down and clearly explained.

Revising the text

Whether you study the novel in a block of time close to the exam or much earlier in your GCSE English literature course, you will need to revise thoroughly if you are to achieve the very best grade that you can.

Reading this guide should, of course, never be a substitute for reading *Animal Farm* itself, but it can help. You should first remind yourself of what happens in the novel, and for this the chapter on 'Plot and structure' might be revisited in the first instance. You might then look at the 'Assessment Objectives and skills' section to ensure that you understand what the examiners are, in general, looking for.

'Tackling the exams' then gives you useful information on the exams and on question format, depending on which examination board specification you are following. It also gives advice on the examination format, and practical considerations such as the time available for the question and the Assessment Objectives that apply to it.

Advice is also supplied on how to approach the question, writing a quick plan and 'working' with the text. AQA and Edexcel both use an essay-type question for *Animal Farm*, while OCR partially uses an extract-based approach for its question on the novel. Focused advice on how you might improve your grade follows, and you need to read this section carefully.

You will find examples of exam-style responses in the 'Sample essays' section, with an examiner's comments in the margins so that you can see clearly how to move towards a Grade 5, and how then to move from a Grade 5 to a Grade 8. When looking at the sample answers, bear in mind that the way responses are assessed is similar (but not identical) across the boards. It is sensible to look online at the sample questions and materials from the particular board that you are taking, and to try planning answers to as many questions as possible. You might also have fun inventing and answering additional questions, since you can be sure that the ones in the sample materials will not be the ones you see when you open the exam paper!

This guide should help you to clarify your thinking about the novel, but it is not a substitute for your thoughtful reading and discussion of *Animal Farm*. The guide should also help you consolidate your approach to writing well under the pressure of the examination. The suggestions in the guide can help you to develop habits of planning and writing answers that take the worry out of *how* you write, and so enable you to concentrate on *what* you write.

The guide is intended to complement the work you do with your teacher, not to replace it. At the end of the main sections there are 'Review your learning' questions to support your thinking. There are 'Build critical skills' and 'Grade booster' boxes at various points; these help you to develop the critical and analytical skills you need to achieve a higher grade. There is also a 'Top ten' quotations section, for characters, top moments and themes. Now that all GCSE literature examinations are 'closed book', this 'Top ten' section will prove helpful in learning short quotations to support points about characters and themes, as well as being a revision aid that identifies the top ten key moments in *Animal Farm*.

When writing about the novel, use this guide as a springboard to develop your own ideas. You should not read this guide in order to memorise chunks of it, ready to regurgitate in the exam. Examiners are not looking for set responses; identical answers are dull. They would like to see that

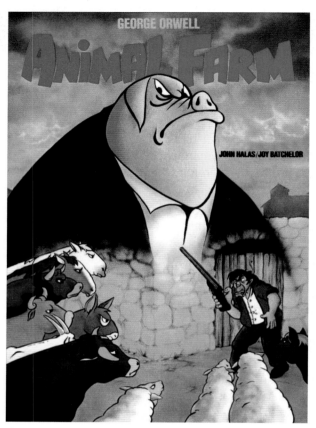

▲ Poster for the 1954 film version, with Napoleon at the centre

you have used everything you have been taught – including by this guide – as a starting point for your own thinking. The examiners hope to reward you for perceptive thought, individual appreciation and varying interpretations. Try to show that you have engaged with the themes and ideas in the novel and that you have explored Orwell's methods with an awareness of the context in which he wrote. Above all, don't be afraid to make it clear that you have enjoyed the novel.

Watching *Animal Farm*

There have been two film adaptations of *Animal Farm*: one produced in 1954 and another in 1999. The first – a cartoon animation – was Britain's first animated feature film and has received much attention as a result of this, along with revelations that its funding came from the CIA (Central Intelligence Agency), which wanted to fund anti-communist art.

The 1999 film incorporates real actors alongside animals, aided by modern technology and digital animation. Neither film is entirely faithful to the original novel, with some changes made to both events and characters, so take care not to get confused if you do watch them. Nevertheless, both films are worth viewing in order to see how events and characters have been interpreted.

Alongside films of the novel, play scripts and stage adaptations exist, so it would be beneficial for you to keep an eye out for any local or national companies staging a production of *Animal Farm*. Ian Wooldridge and Peter Hall's play scripts of the novel offer an interesting comparison for you, and can be read quite easily alongside the original novel.

You will find interesting differences from the text in these adaptations. Bear in mind that while they are enjoyable versions of the tale and convey the essential message of the novel, they should never be seen as a substitute for the text itself. Examiners are unlikely to be impressed by responses that refer to the film versions rather than the novel itself.

Enjoy referring to the guide as you study the text, and good luck in your exam.

Target your thinking

- What is meant by 'context'? (**AO3**)
- What does the context of the novel tell us about its purpose? (**AO3**)
- How did Orwell's life experiences influence his novel? (**AO3**)
- How does Orwell relate the events in the novel to those in the real world? (**AO3**)

What is meant by 'context'?

Knowledge of context will help you understand and appreciate your reading of *Animal Farm*, but what exactly does this mean?

The context of a text refers to the circumstances at the time the text was written – in other words the historical, socio-economic and political circumstances at the time, as well as the author's beliefs about those circumstances. It also refers to the way that more personal events in the author's own life may have influenced his or her thinking and writing. Finally, context may refer to literary context and be concerned with developments in the novel as a form that may also have influenced the way it was written. *Animal Farm* was published in 1945, the same year World War II ended. Alongside *Nineteen Eighty-Four*, it is one of Orwell's most famous works. Understanding the man behind the book, as well as political events in Britain and the world at the time the book was written, will help you grasp the context of the novel.

Orwell's life

Early life and education

George Orwell's real name was Eric Arthur Blair. He was born in India in 1903. India was part of the British Empire at the time, and his father worked there as an agent in the Indian Civil Service. Orwell came from a middle-class family and led a relatively privileged life.

When Orwell was eight years old, his family returned to England and his parents sent him to a private prep school. His experiences there, which he recounts in his autobiographical essay *Such, Such Were the Joys*, may have shaped his beliefs about the ease with which authority may be abused, which is a key theme in *Animal Farm*.

On leaving school, he joined the Indian Imperial Police but found it unsuitable and soon resigned.

▲ George Orwell

Life as a writer

Orwell's disenchantment with the way Britain ruled India was an early indication of his future as a political writer.

Orwell returned to England in the spring of 1928, spurred on by the disgust and guilt he felt at his background and the imperialism of which he had been a part. He decided to live in poverty, in London and Paris; these experiences resulted in his book *Down and Out in Paris and London*, which was published in 1933. In this book, Orwell sought to educate the English middle class about the way in which the life they led and enjoyed was founded upon the exploitation of those from whom they distanced themselves. He viewed himself as part of the English moral conscience and his writings reflected this.

It was at this stage that Eric Blair took on the pseudonym George Orwell. Perhaps it was his way of shedding his old identity and taking on a new one. Unable to support himself with his writing, however, Orwell took up a teaching post at a private school. Later he was commissioned to produce a documentary account of unemployment in the north of England for the Left Book Club, a left-wing organisation that sought to 'help in the struggle for world peace and against fascism'. *The Road to Wigan Pier* was published in 1937 and is viewed as a milestone in modern literary journalism. In *The Road to Wigan Pier*, Orwell writes of his desire to 'escape from … every form of man's dominion over man' and comments on the social structures that encourage 'dominion over others'.

The Spanish Civil War

Orwell went to Spain in order to write newspaper articles on the **Civil War**. When he arrived he initially found that class distinctions appeared to have vanished and, while there was a shortage of everything, there *was* equality.

Socialism appeared to be a real possibility, something worth fighting for, so Orwell joined in the struggle and was sent to the front. He became disillusioned, however, with the rivalry between the **communists** and other **factions** fighting the **fascists**. When he returned to Barcelona, he found that society had reverted to the previous situation of inequality. From his experiences in Spain, Orwell learned that socialism in action was only a temporary possibility. It confirmed for him that modern society cannot exist without different classes and that there is something in human nature that will always seek violence, conflict and power over others – which results in inequality and abuse, as can be seen in *Animal Farm*. His book *Homage to Catalonia* is an account of the civil war in Spain.

Spanish Civil War (1936–39): war in which Nationalist forces led by Franco rose against the Republican government of Spain, with various left-wing groups fighting on the Republican side. Franco was established as a fascist dictator and ruled until his death in 1975.

Socialism: an economic system based on collective ownership (usually state ownership of money and industry).

Communism: a form of socialism that abolishes private ownership; all property is held in common, actual ownership being ascribed to the community as a whole or to the state.

It became clear that while Orwell was a socialist, his experiences in life had led him to become disillusioned; when the fascism of Hitler and Mussolini was given the ironic title of 'national socialism', Orwell began to fear that socialism would become fascism. This is seen in *Animal Farm* in the way that the socialist rebellion against the humans later gives way to a fascist dictatorship under the pigs.

Novel writing

At the outbreak of war in 1939, Orwell tried to join the army but he was declared physically unfit. Therefore he served in the Home Guard and worked as a journalist.

Towards the end of the war, Orwell wrote *Animal Farm: A Fairy Story*. After initial difficulties getting the novel published, it enjoyed great success despite the shortage of paper at the time in the UK and USA. It was translated into many languages around the world and brought Orwell worldwide fame.

He wrote his best known work, *Nineteen Eighty-Four*, in 1948 (see the connection?) and it was published the following year. This was written as a warning against the state taking complete control over its citizens, so creating a **totalitarian** dictatorship. In the novel the god-like leader, Big Brother, has created a cult of personality. There are cameras *everywhere*, including in every room of every house. Hence the famous slogan used throughout the novel: 'Big Brother is watching you.' (The term 'Big Brother' and this slogan have entered popular culture, for instance in the title of the reality TV show.) A new language has been created, Newspeak, to control what the people think and to limit freedom of thought. (You will meet these concepts of totalitarianism, personality cult and controlling citizens' thoughts in *Animal Farm*.)

Orwell died from tuberculosis in London on 21 January 1950.

Faction: members of a group or organisation who hold views not representative of the wider group.
Fascism: a governmental system led by a dictator who has complete power and who forcibly suppresses opposition and criticism, ensuring all industry, commerce, etc., is centralised; usually emphasises an aggressive nationalism and often racism.
Totalitarianism: a form of government that demands total obedience to the state and aims for complete control over all aspects of public and private life.

GRADE BOOSTER

Knowing about how Orwell's background influenced his writing of *Animal Farm*, as well as the context of the novel, is important as it will help you understand the author's purposes and concerns. While this information should help you write more confidently about the novel, there is little to be gained by simply 'bolting on' biographical details; they must always be related closely to the question you are answering and used sparingly.

The Soviet Union

The events in *Animal Farm* can be seen to relate to those in Russia between 1917 and 1943, therefore you need to know a bit of Russian history in order to discuss some of the novel's themes.

Tsar: a king/emperor.
Bolshevik: a left-wing majority group that followed Lenin; it eventually became the Russian Communist Party.

For centuries Russia was ruled by **tsars**, who had total authority. Tsar Nicholas II ruled from 1894. Under the reign of the tsars, the ruling classes lived in luxury while the rest of the population suffered, in the same way that, in the novel, Jones lives happily while the animals suffer. Despite the desire for social and political change (shown by minor revolts and the formation of political organisations), however, it was not until 1917 and the shortages and other hardships of World War I, that increased dissatisfaction and rebellion led to the February Revolution. In February 1917, the **Bolsheviks** forced Tsar Nicholas II to abdicate his position as leader of Russia. The nation's imperial rule under the Romanov dynasty ended, in a similar way to Jones being ousted from Manor Farm.

After the tsar's abdication an ineffective provisional government ran Russia, until Vladimir Lenin (a Bolshevik leader) returned from exile. Helped by Leon Trotsky (another former exile) and Joseph Stalin, Lenin launched a successful takeover against the provisional government. On 25 October 1917, as a result of the October Revolution, a new government based on the tenets of communism was founded. In the same way, the animals in the novel establish a farm based on the ideals of 'Animalism'.

Lenin's rise to power did not lead to further success or popularity. Russia's former privileged classes, as well as its working and farming classes, became dissatisfied with the new government and they started to enlist foreign support for their cause. As a result, the White Army (aided by Britain and France) and the Red Army (led by Trotsky) were formed. In the novel, Jones's alliances with neighbouring farmers and the animals' battles against the humans, in particular the Battle of the Cowshed, mirror these events.

Russia's civil war lasted until 1921, and in 1922 the Union of Soviet Socialist Republics (USSR) was created. In 1924, however, Lenin, who had been leading the USSR, died. This left Trotsky and Stalin, both power-hungry politicians, to battle for Russia's leadership. In the same way, in the novel, Snowball and Napoleon are seen to battle over leadership of Animal Farm.

Despite Trotsky's ability as an orator, he was unable to defeat Stalin, who had the help of important internal alliances. Stalin exiled Trotsky, along with many other leaders, in the Great Purge, and eventually he had Trotsky assassinated in Mexico. For the next 25 years, Stalin was the leader of the Soviet Union. In a similar way, Napoleon expels Snowball in order to rule the farm.

◀ Lenin (left) and Stalin in 1922

Russia suffered long-standing economic deficiencies and many losses as a result of World War I. In an effort to improve the situation, Stalin launched several Five Year Plans – aggressive campaigns to increase the country's productivity while bringing the economy completely under government control. These ideas had originally been suggested by Trotsky in his efforts to industrialise Russia, but had been dismissed by Stalin who had wanted to focus on building up defences. In an about-face, however, he now adopted these ideas. Similarly, in the novel Napoleon takes up Snowball's idea to build a windmill after initially ridiculing it.

These plans were successful but resulted in dissatisfaction among the citizens of the Soviet Union, particularly the land-owning peasants who did not want their farms to be placed under government control. In order to prevent them rebelling, Stalin used a carefully organised terror campaign. He began a series of 'purges' in which he killed anyone suspected of harbouring ideas that went against his own. He was determined to protect himself from treachery, so he increased the government's internal espionage, using the Secret Police, and he turned citizens against one another.

Russian people were terrified of being imprisoned, tortured or sent to work in the Soviet labour camps. They also feared being executed, so they spied on and turned in their co-workers, neighbours and even family members. Tens of millions were slaughtered. This created a climate of fear in which Stalin had absolute control over Soviet society. Very similar events happen on Animal Farm: animals are seen to confess to crimes and are slaughtered as a result, and Napoleon controls the whole farm.

Stalin now focused his attention on international affairs. Feeling that Russia was isolated and at risk from outside forces, Stalin signed a non-aggression pact with Germany in 1939. In *Animal Farm*, Napoleon's trading with Frederick mirrors this event. During World War II, however, Germany broke the non-aggression pact and invaded the Soviet Union. In *Animal Farm*, the Battle of the Windmill represents this invasion. The war took a terrible toll on the Soviet Union and in 1943 Britain agreed to aid Russia against Hitler; the final section of *Animal Farm* represents the conference that took place in Tehran to negotiate this aid. Despite harsh battles and the loss of more than 20 million citizens, the Soviet Union managed to drive the Nazis out and continued marching westward, seizing control of Berlin in May 1945.

A few months later, George Orwell published *Animal Farm*, allegorically recounting much of this history. Stalin remained in control of the Soviet Union until his death in 1953. Orwell found it very difficult to get the novel published, however, due to the political relationship between Russia and the UK. At this time Stalin was held in high regard in Britain – he was often referred to as 'Uncle Joe'. Russia was Britain's ally in World War II, helping to defeat Nazi Germany. A Ministry of Information official told one publisher that it was 'highly ill-advised to publish [*Animal Farm*] at the present time'. Orwell, however, was determined to question the prevailing public and establishment view that demanded an uncritical admiration of Soviet Russia.

Although the central idea for the novel may have sprung from Orwell's experience of the Spanish Civil War and events in Russia, the actual details of the story did not come to him for some time. One day he saw a young boy, perhaps ten years old, driving a huge cart-horse along a narrow path, whipping it whenever it tried to turn. It struck Orwell that if only such animals became aware of their strength, humans should have no power over them, and that men exploit animals in much the same way as the rich exploit the **proletariat**.

Proletariat: working class/lower class.

Awareness of context

Compare the following sets of responses from students who are working at higher and lower levels (see page opposite). Notice how the better candidate has successfully integrated their awareness of context.

> **GRADE** *BOOSTER*
>
> You will not be assessed on context separately, but it is a sign of a high-level response if it incorporates relevant contextual information.

Lower-level responses	Higher-level responses
Napoleon becomes a dictator and kills animals on the farm.	Napoleon betrays the ideals of Animalism and starts to kill any animals on the farm who express anti-Napoleon sentiments, mirroring Stalin's purges in Russia when he staged 'show trials', in which people confessed to supposed crimes only to be publicly killed.
Events on the farm show the way in which people want power over each other.	The novel was written as an allegory of events in Russia and demonstrates Orwell's belief that while socialism is possible for a brief time, man will always seek power over others.
Events in the book can be linked with Russian history. Napoleon and Snowball fight to control the farm but Napoleon wins.	The battle between Snowball and Napoleon symbolises the way that Trotsky and Stalin fought for control of Russia after Lenin's death.
Mr Jones is a typical human, wanting to boss the animals around. He is like the tsar in Russia.	Mr Jones represents the ruling class in Russia during the Romanov dynasty, in particular Tsar Nicholas II.

REVIEW YOUR LEARNING

(Answers are given on p. 102.)

1 What was George Orwell's real name and why might he have changed it?

2 How might his experience of the Spanish Civil War have influenced his writing?

3 Can you think of a thematic link between *Animal Farm* and *Nineteen Eighty-Four*?

4 Give two ways in which *Animal Farm* parallels Russian history.

5 Offer one reason why Orwell had difficulty getting *Animal Farm* published.

GRADE *FOCUS*

Grade 5
To achieve a Grade 5, students will show a clear understanding of the context in which the novel was written.

Grade 8
To achieve a Grade 8, students will make perceptive, critical comments about the ways contextual factors affect the choices that the writer makes.

Plot and structure

Target your thinking

- What are the main events of the novel? (**AO1**)
- How do the main storylines develop through the novel? (**AO1, AO2**)
- How do these events correspond with Russian history? (**AO1, AO2**)
- How does Orwell organise these events? (**AO2**)

Plot

Chapter 1

Build critical skills

Think about the importance of the opening chapter of *Animal Farm*. What do you think is the purpose of this chapter?

Manor Farm, where the novel is set, is owned by Mr Jones, a drunken, boorish farmer. Orwell introduces Mr Jones in the first sentence as a neglectful farmer who drinks too much and is too drunk to shut the openings to the hen-houses. Once he goes to sleep, the animals are described as 'stirring' and 'fluttering', suggesting an excitement of anticipation because old Major, the prize-winning white boar, has called a meeting in the barn in which he plans to tell the animals of his dream. Old Major is described as a 'highly regarded' pig and as such the animals are willing to lose some sleep in order to hear his dream.

In the barn, the main characters who will feature in the rest of the novel are introduced: Boxer the cart-horse; Clover the motherly mare; Mollie the mare who pulls Jones's trap; Benjamin the donkey; Muriel the goat; Moses the raven. Orwell introduces us to the animals – some by breed, some by name – and the reader gains an impression of their characters from his descriptions, for example Clover makes a wall around the ducklings with her 'great foreleg' to protect them.

Old Major talks about Man's tyranny over animals and suggests that animals are miserable and work as slaves, then are killed. He says that all they produce is taken by humans and that Man is the only animal who tyrannises and consumes without producing. Old Major suggests that the only solution is rebellion against Man. He establishes that all men are enemies and all animals are comrades, and he goes on to describe an ideal future time when animals will live in freedom. He then says that the following rules, which later form the basis of Animalism, must be remembered:

- Animals must never resemble Man.
- Animals must never live in a house, lie in a bed, wear clothes, drink alcohol, use tobacco, touch money or engage in trade.

Key quotation

'No animal in England is free'

Key quotation

'The life of an animal is misery and slavery'

- No animal must tyrannise another.
- No animal must kill another.
- All animals are equal.

Old Major then teaches the animals a song called 'Beasts of England', which his mother had taught him and he remembered in his dream. It talks of a 'golden future time' and the animals join in singing it five times in succession! Their singing wakes Jones, however, and we then see the tight grip he has on the animals. Jones's brutal response is to fire the gun which, Orwell cleverly points out, 'always stood in the corner of his bedroom', implying the violence with which Jones ruled his farm and his lack of concern for the animals' welfare. The gunshot results in the animals' swift silence: 'the whole farm was asleep in a moment'.

Build critical skills

The song that the animals sing presents an idealised vision of the future. List the ways in which the words in the song do this.

▲ The animals sing 'Beasts of England'

Chapter 2

Three nights later, old Major dies peacefully in his sleep. The animals secretly plot a rebellion, with the work of teaching and organising falling to the pigs, the most intelligent animals. Napoleon, a determined pig with a reputation for getting his own way, and Snowball, a vivacious and inventive pig, take the lead. Together with Squealer, a pig who was a 'brilliant talker', they formulate the principles of Animalism, a philosophy based on old Major's teachings. They spread this among the other animals but many find the principles difficult to understand, as they have grown up believing that Mr Jones is their natural and rightful master.

Build critical skills

Although old Major talks about animals being equal, there are early indications that they are not. What signs are there of this in Chapter 1? Why does Orwell include these early indications?

Key quotation

Napoleon: 'Not much of a talker, but with a reputation for getting his own way.'

Key quotation

Snowball: 'Quicker in speech and more inventive'

Key quotation

Snowball: 'Twinkling eyes, nimble movements, and a shrill voice. He was a brilliant talker.'

Build critical skills

The animals are presented as victors after the humans are banished. How does Orwell's choice of words, when he describes the animals' celebrations, suggest this?

Build critical skills

It is clear that Mollie has early reservations about life without humans. What signs are there of this?

Moses tempts the animals with stories of 'Sugarcandy Mountain', an idyllic place situated in the sky. Many animals hate Moses for his tale-telling and laziness, but some believe in Sugarcandy Mountain, a representation of Heaven, and the pigs work hard to dispel the myth of its existence.

We are told that although Mr Jones had been a 'capable farmer', he had always been a 'hard master'. With drink, he had become neglectful. It is this neglect and the animals' lack of feeding that starts off a chain of events that leads to the sudden and unplanned Rebellion. The humans are shocked at 'the sudden uprising of creatures whom they were used to thrashing and maltreating just as they chose', so much so that it 'frightened them almost out of their wits'. They panic, take to their heels and are driven off the farm 'in full flight', with Mrs Jones hurriedly flinging a few possessions in a bag.

GRADE BOOSTER

Boxer and Clover are described as hard workers and loyal supporters of Animalism. Recognising that this heightens our reaction to the cruel way Boxer is treated later in the novel will show that you are aware of Orwell as an author who is in complete control of his writing.

Once the humans are banished, the animals set about eliminating all reminders of Jones, and with all badges of slavery removed the animals are seen to rejoice, indulging in double rations and singing 'Beasts of England' contentedly, 'seven times running'.

The next day, the animals wake up to a new dawn and, after surveying the farm, they explore the farmhouse, from where Mollie takes a ribbon, only to be chastised by the others. The animals decide that no animal shall ever live in the farmhouse and that it should be preserved as a museum.

After breakfast, the pigs tell the others that they have taught themselves to write. Snowball writes the new name of the farm, 'Animal Farm', in place of Manor Farm, and with Squealer's help he writes the principles of Animalism, which the pigs have reduced to seven 'unalterable' commandments. They state:

- Whatever goes upon two legs is an enemy.
- Whatever goes upon four legs, or has wings, is a friend.
- No animal shall wear clothes.
- No animal shall sleep in a bed.
- No animal shall drink alcohol.
- No animal shall kill any other animal.
- All animals are equal.

▲ Snowball and the animals' commandments

Shortly afterwards, it becomes apparent that the cows need to be milked. The pigs manage to do this and Napoleon tells the others to follow Snowball to the harvest. When they return, the milk has disappeared.

The interval between old Major's death and the Rebellion signifies the long period in history when socialism grew. Following the deaths of Karl Marx and Friedrich Engels in 1883 and 1895 respectively, political ideas developed and the working classes grew more educated and started to want more from life. (See p. 37 for more about Marx and Engels.)

Orwell develops our understanding of the three main pigs in this chapter and draws distinctions between all the animals' views of the new system. He also introduces the idea of organised religion through Moses and indicates the suspicious way it is viewed. This is in keeping with Marx's view of organised religion as the 'opiate of the masses'. He believed it prevented people from changing their lives for the better by encouraging them to accept their unhappy situation in the belief that everlasting happiness was awaiting them in Heaven.

At the end of the chapter Orwell indicates the way in which the ideals of Animalism will be broken when the milk vanishes while the animals are working.

Chapter 3

The animals work very hard and, despite using instruments created for humans, the harvest is completed in two days fewer than it had taken Jones and his men, and is the biggest the farm has seen.

Key quotation

'All through the summer the work of the farm went like clockwork'

The pigs do not work but direct others, assuming leadership of the farm. In contrast, Boxer gets up earlier than the others and works harder than ever, adopting the motto of 'I will work harder' when faced with difficulties. Meanwhile, the cat and Mollie shirk work and Benjamin remains his cynical self.

On Sundays, there is no work, breakfast is an hour later and the animals meet for a ceremony involving the hoisting of a flag – a green tablecloth with a hoof and horn painted on it – and a Meeting in the barn, where the forthcoming week is discussed.

Only the pigs make resolutions but Snowball and Napoleon constantly disagree. It is agreed, however, that the small paddock behind the orchard should be a resting place for retired animals, although Snowball and Napoleon fail to agree on a retiring age for each type of animal.

Snowball sets up a number of Animal Committees, most of which fail. His educational initiatives prove more successful, however, with most animals gaining some degree of literacy. Benjamin learns to read as well as the pigs, but Boxer cannot get beyond the letter D in the alphabet. To make things easier, Snowball simplifies the Seven Commandments to 'Four legs good, two legs bad' for the benefit of the less intelligent animals, and the sheep learn and repeat this maxim for hours on end.

Napoleon takes no interest in Snowball's committees, instead seeing education of the young as a priority. He takes Jessie and Bluebell's nine puppies, saying that he will take responsibility for their education, and installs them in the loft, which is inaccessible to others.

It is revealed that the milk that vanished in Chapter 2 is being mixed into the pigs' mash, and when the apples ripen they too are taken to the harness room for the pigs' use. Squealer explains to the other animals that milk and apples are necessary for pigs because they are 'brain-workers' and he suggests that without them the pigs could fail in protecting the animals from the return of Mr Jones. All the animals agree that this would be a bad thing.

Key quotation

'Snowball busied himself organising the ... Animal Committees'

Key quotation

'Napoleon ... said that ... the education of the young was more important'

Build critical skills

Why does Napoleon focus on educating the young and what are his reasons for taking the puppies?

Key quotation

'The importance of keeping the pigs in good health was all too obvious'

GRADE BOOSTER

Recognising, where appropriate, in your responses that Squealer's manipulation represents political rhetoric – the indoctrination of the uneducated – will show that you understand how the novel is satirical.

At the end of the chapter Orwell indicates the way in which the ideals will be broken. The taking of the milk is the first, and therefore a very important, indication that even at this early stage in the Rebellion, the ideals of Animal Farm will not be achieved.

In this chapter, Orwell highlights the differences between Snowball and Napoleon. Snowball busies himself with organising the work of the farm, while Napoleon starts to develop his power base, looking towards the future when he will use the dogs to secure his control. This parallels the contrast between Trotsky and Stalin, with Trotsky focusing on organising Workers' Committees to educate the illiterate Russian masses and teach them about communism, and Stalin establishing his power base. Squealer's role as the voice of media and propaganda is also established in this chapter.

Chapter 4

By late summer, news of the Rebellion has spread across half the county. Mr Jones spends most of his time in the Red Lion Pub, drinking and complaining about his misfortune. His neighbours, Mr Pilkington of Foxwood Farm and Mr Frederick of Pinchfield Farm, fear their own animals will follow those on Manor Farm, but their rivalry with each other prevents them from working together against Animal Farm. Instead, they refuse to recognise Animal Farm's new name and spread false rumours about the farm's inefficiency and immorality. Meanwhile, pigeons sent by Napoleon and Snowball spread news of the Rebellion and teach animals 'Beasts of England', so that many of the animals on other farms begin to behave rebelliously.

Finally, in early October, Mr Jones and some of Pilkington's and Frederick's men attempt to seize control of Animal Farm. A flight of pigeons alerts the other animals of this and Snowball, who has studied books about the battle campaigns of Julius Caesar, leads the animals in an ambush. Boxer and Snowball fight courageously and the humans are ejected quickly, with victory falling to the animals.

The animals lose only a sheep, which is given a hero's burial. Thinking that he has unintentionally killed a stable boy (who is later discovered to have fled), Boxer expresses his regret at taking a life. Snowball's attitude is the complete opposite, however, and he reassures Boxer, stating that 'the only good human being is a dead one'.

Mollie's ability to shirk is seen again, as she is found hiding in her stall after the battle. Snowball and Boxer each receive medals inscribed with the words 'Animal Hero, First Class'. The animals decide to call the battle the 'Battle of the Cowshed'. After discovering Mr Jones's gun where he dropped it in the mud, they place this at the base of the flagstaff, agreeing to fire it twice a year: on 12 October, the anniversary of the battle, and on Midsummer's Day, the anniversary of the Rebellion.

Key quotation

'"He is dead," said Boxer sorrowfully'

Key quotation

Snowball: 'War is war. The only good human being is a dead one'

In this chapter, Orwell draws parallels between the attempt by the pigs to spread Animalism and the efforts of the early followers of communism to spread its ideas. Just as the West refused to cooperate politically with the USSR, in this chapter Pilkington and Frederick refuse to recognise Animal Farm. Also, the West's financial and military aid to the White Army – old supporters of the tsarist regime – is symbolised by Orwell in the Battle of the Cowshed. The higher status assumed by the pigs in terms of rations indicates the way in which ideals are being broken. The growing conflict between Napoleon and Snowball is also highlighted.

Chapter 5

As winter draws on, it becomes apparent that Mollie is becoming more and more difficult. She arrives late for work, accepts treats from men linked with nearby farms, and generally behaves in a way contrary to the principles of Animalism. Eventually she disappears and the pigeons later report that she has been lured away by a fat, red-faced man who strokes her coat and feeds her sugar and that she now pulls his carriage.

During the cold winter months, the animals continue to hold their Meetings in the barn, and Snowball and Napoleon continue to disagree over issues. It is evident that Snowball is the better speaker, but that Napoleon is better at gaining support between Meetings.

Snowball is ambitious for the farm. He studies Mr Jones's books and is full of ideas for making improvements. These include a scheme to build a windmill, from which the animals can generate electricity, thus reducing the burden on them. Napoleon, however, asserts that building the windmill will entail a lot of hard work and difficulty and that the animals should concentrate on greater food production, rather than plan for a distant future. He places greater importance on securing the farm by procuring firearms and training animals to use them, while Snowball thinks it better to stir up rebellion in other farms so that defending Animal Farm is not needed. The animals are divided and Napoleon is contemptuous of Snowball's initial plans for the windmill.

Key quotation

'None of the other animals ever mentions Mollie again.'

Build critical skills

What reasons might the animals have for never mentioning Mollie again?

When Snowball's windmill plans are finalised, all the animals assemble for a great Meeting to vote on whether to carry out the project. Snowball gives a powerful speech, but Napoleon's response is just thirty seconds long and dismissive. When Snowball speaks further, inspiring the animals with his descriptions of the wonders of electricity, the animals are moved to side with him, but just as they prepare to vote, Napoleon gives a strange whimper and nine enormous dogs charge into the barn. They attack Snowball, chasing him off the farm.

When the dogs return to their master's side, Napoleon announces that henceforth Meetings will be held only for ceremonial purposes. All important decisions will fall to the pigs.

Many of the animals feel confused and disturbed by these events, but Squealer placates them. He explains that Napoleon is making a great sacrifice in taking responsibility for leadership and that, as the cleverest animal, he serves the interests of all of them. The animals still question the expulsion of Snowball but Squealer explains that Snowball was a traitor and a criminal. Despite initial reservations, eventually the animals come to accept this version of events, especially when they are threatened with the return of Jones. Boxer adds 'Napoleon is always right' to his other motto, 'I will work harder'.

In Sunday Meetings now, Napoleon and the other pigs take to sitting on a raised platform, from where they issue their orders. Three weeks after Snowball's banishment, the animals learn that Napoleon, in fact, supports the windmill project. Squealer explains that he never really opposed it. He just pretended to in order to expel the disloyal Snowball. These tactics, according to Squealer, served to advance the interest of all the animals. Squealer's words, combined with the threatening growls of Napoleon's three dogs, convince the animals to accept his explanation without question.

Build critical skills

Propaganda is the deliberate spreading of ideas or information, true or untrue, with the purpose of manipulating public opinion to gain support for one's cause or to discourage support for an opposing cause. Squealer acts as the voice of propaganda. Identify examples of how he does this in this chapter and explain why he uses propaganda in each case.

In this chapter, Mollie represents those Russians who defected to the West in search of a better life and more personal freedom. Also in this chapter, Orwell draws parallels between Napoleon and Snowball's differences and Stalin and Trotsky's disagreements over organisation and industrial development. Stalin wanted to make Russia as powerful and advanced as the West and drove Trotsky out of Russia, helped by the

Key quotation

Napoleon: '...suddenly he lifted his leg, urinated over the plans, and walked out without uttering a word.'

Build critical skills

How does Orwell show that the dogs represent the Secret Police? Think about how the dogs act, how the other animals react to them and how Orwell refers to them.

Key quotation

'It was noticed that they wagged their tails to him in the same way as the other dogs had been used to do to Mr Jones.'

Key quotation

Boxer: 'Napoleon is always right' and 'I will work harder'

▲ Propaganda poster from 1931: 'The USSR is the shock battalion of the world proletariat!'

Russian Secret Police (Trotsky was murdered in Mexico, on Stalin's orders, in 1940).

Minimus's inclusion indicates the way that Communist Russia used art and literature to promote its values. The rewriting of history begins in this chapter, with Squealer stating that Napoleon was never against the windmill.

Chapter 6

The animals work like slaves doing a 60-hour week. In August, Napoleon announces that the animals are also to work on Sunday afternoons. This work is 'voluntary', but the animals will receive no food unless they carry it out.

The animals are loyal to the farm and believe what the pigs tell them, so they commit themselves to the extra work. Boxer, in particular, toils very hard, doing the work of three horses but never complaining. Despite having all the necessary materials to build the windmill, they struggle to break the stone into usable sizes. Once they learn to raise and then drop big stones into the quarry, however, they succeed in smashing them into easier chunks and finally solve this problem. By late summer, they have enough broken stone to begin construction.

Although the animals' work is exhausting, they do not suffer any more than they had done under Mr Jones. They have enough to eat and can maintain the farm grounds easily now that humans no longer take their produce. The farm still needs items that it cannot produce itself, however, such as iron, nails and paraffin. When existing supplies of these begin to run low, Napoleon announces a new policy of trading with neighbouring farms. Despite some animals' misgivings and vague recollections that they had agreed not to do this, the dogs' growling and Napoleon's reassurances that all arrangements have been made, along with Squealer's talks afterwards, make the animals believe they are mistaken.

Mr Whymper, a human solicitor, is hired to assist Napoleon to conduct trade on behalf of Animal Farm. He begins to visit the farm every Monday and Napoleon places orders with him for various supplies.

Key quotation

'All that year the animals worked like slaves'

Key quotation

'Afterwards Squealer made a round of the farm and set the animals' minds at rest.'

The pigs start to live in the farmhouse and it is rumoured that they sleep in beds, a violation of the Fourth Commandment. When Clover asks Muriel to read her the commandment, however, they find that it now reads, 'No animal shall sleep in a bed *with sheets.*'

According to Squealer, Clover must have forgotten the last two words. He assures the animals that a pile of straw is a bed and that they all therefore sleep in beds. Sheets, he says, as a human invention, are the true source of evil. He emotionally blackmails the animals into agreeing that the pigs need proper rest in order to think clearly and to serve the best interests of the farm.

In November, a terrible storm hits Animal Farm, knocking down the windmill, among other things. The animals are devastated but Napoleon blames this on Snowball, who, he says, will do anything to destroy Animal Farm. He passes a death sentence on Snowball, offering a bushel of apples to anyone who kills him. He then gives an impassioned speech in which he convinces the animals that they must rebuild the windmill.

In this chapter, Orwell draws a parallel between the building of the windmill and Stalin's first Five Year Plan. The struggles that the animals face represent the difficulties faced by Russia in developing as an industrial nation. We see in this chapter the power and control that the pigs now have over the other animals. Orwell suggests the slow deterioration in conditions, with the animals being treated as they were in Jones's time. Things begin to return to what they once were: the farm trades and the pigs start to become the elite, moving in to the farmhouse. Fear is seen as a control mechanism, just as it was in Communist Russia; Squealer always has the dogs with him when trying to persuade the animals. This is the first chapter in which a commandment is changed.

> **Key quotation**
>
> *Napoleon: "Do you know the enemy who has come in the night and overthrown our windmill? SNOWBALL!" He suddenly roared in a voice of thunder.'*

Chapter 7

The winter is bitter, and snow, sleet and frost hamper the animals as they struggle to rebuild the windmill. The humans refuse to believe that Snowball was behind the destruction of the windmill, claiming instead that the windmill's walls were not thick enough. Despite stating that this is false, the animals decide to build the windmill walls twice as thick.

When the animals fall short of food in January and face possible starvation, rumours of famine and disease spread. To counter this, Napoleon has Mr Whymper visit the farm and tricks him into thinking that rations have been increased and that the grain stores are full.

To feed the animals, Napoleon decides to sell 400 eggs per week. The animals are shocked, believing that one of old Major's original complaints against humans centred on the cruelty of egg-selling. When the hens rebel by smashing their eggs, Napoleon starves them out by cutting their rations entirely. Nine hens die before the others submit to Napoleon's demands.

> **Key quotation**
>
> *'It was a bitter winter.'*

Key quotation

'For the first time since the expulsion of Jones there was something resembling a rebellion.'

Key quotation

Squealer: '...it was noticed he cast a very ugly look at Boxer with his little twinkling eyes'

Build critical skills

How does Orwell signify at this point that something might happen to Boxer later? What is the effect on the reader?

Build critical skills

One of Napoleon's tactics is to use Squealer to spread false rumours about Snowball and so start the process of rewriting history. Find and list other examples of Orwell showing that Animal Farm's history is being rewritten.

Key quotation

'...there was a pile of corpses lying before Napoleon's feet and the air was heavy with the smell of blood'

Squealer vividly rewrites events at the Battle of the Cowshed, claiming that Napoleon was the hero at the battle, and stating that Napoleon has said 'categorically that Snowball was Jones's agent from the very beginning'. The animals are astonished at what Squealer says about Snowball, especially Boxer who is completely bemused, recalling the medal Snowball was given, but Squealer's description is so vivid that even Boxer finally agrees to this version of events.

Four days later, Napoleon calls all the animals into the yard. With his dogs around him, he forces specific animals to confess their participation in a conspiracy with Snowball. The dogs tear out the throats of these 'traitors' and then, seemingly without orders, they attack Boxer, who effortlessly kicks them away with his hooves. Four pigs and various other animals are killed, including the hens who rebelled against selling their eggs.

The animals are deeply upset and confused by these events. Once Napoleon leaves, Boxer states that he cannot believe that such a thing could happen on Animal Farm and that he thinks it must result from some fault in the animals. He, therefore, commits to working even harder. Clover, on the other hand, wonders how their glorious Rebellion could have come to this.

When Clover leads some of the animals to sing 'Beasts of England', Squealer appears and explains that 'Beasts of England' is no longer to be sung as it is the song of the Rebellion and now that there is no more need for rebellion, the song is defunct. Squealer presents the animals with a replacement song, written by Minimus, the poet pig, which expresses patriotism and glorifies Animal Farm but does not inspire the animals as much.

In this chapter, Orwell shows how Snowball, like Trotsky, becomes the scapegoat who is blamed for everything and is accused of industrial sabotage. The rewriting of history continues in this chapter, with Snowball's acts in the Battle of the Cowshed being altered. The confessions by the animals are akin to those expressed in the 1930s in the USSR, when Stalin set about removing anyone who appeared to oppose him.

Build critical skills

Seven million Russians were executed or put into labour camps. The killing of the animals represents these purges, as well as the brutality used by dictators more generally in order to maintain their power. What has happened so far in the novel to lead up to this situation? What effect do you think this incident has on the reader and how might it anticipate worse times to come?

When Clover thinks back to the past, Orwell is cleverly reminding us that the ideals of Animalism have been shattered. This is reinforced when the anthem of rebellion is replaced with another song, rich in irony, which fails to inspire the rest of the animals.

Chapter 8

A few days after the trauma of the executions, the animals discover that the Sixth Commandment reads: 'No animal shall kill any other animal *without cause.*' Once again, the animals blame this apparent change in wording on their bad memories. They work even harder to rebuild the windmill, although they suffer from hunger and cold. Squealer continually blinds them with science, citing statistics to prove that conditions on the farm are better than they experienced under Mr Jones and that they continue to improve.

Napoleon is rarely seen and, when he is, he is surrounded by the dogs and his presence is announced by a cockerel. He adopts the title of 'Leader', along with other complimentary names. Orwell shows the gradual erosion of ideals when Napoleon adopts various titles and has a food taster, suggesting the emperor-like status he now holds. Minimus writes a poem in praise of Napoleon, also rich in irony, and inscribes it on the barn wall.

It is at this time that Napoleon enters complicated negotiations to sell some timber. The pigs incite hatred of whichever neighbour appears not to be buying the timber at the time: they encourage the animals to hate Pilkington when negotiations favour Frederick, and vice versa. Snowball is also said to be hiding in whichever farm is currently out of favour. Following great anti-Frederick propaganda, during which Napoleon promotes the maxim 'Death to Frederick!', the animals are shocked to learn that Frederick is the final buyer of timber. Napoleon's cleverness is endlessly praised by the pigs for, rather than accept a cheque for the timber, he insists on receiving cash, which he gets in the form of five pound notes that later turn out to be worthless forgeries.

Napoleon's complex negotiations with neighbouring farmers mirror the attempts by Stalin to broker a deal with Western democracies, and the sale of the timber to Frederick is akin to Stalin's non-aggression pact with Adolf Hitler. The deception of the forged notes is Orwell's method of indicating the way in which Russia was deceived when Germany attacked it in 1941.

Soon the windmill is finished but before they can put it to use, Napoleon discovers that the money Frederick has given him for the timber is fake. Napoleon pronounces a death sentence on Frederick and warns the animals to prepare themselves for the worst.

Key quotation

'Animal Farm, Animal Farm,

Never through me shalt thou come to harm.'

Key quotation

'Every beast great or small,

Sleeps at peace in his stall,

Thou watchest over all,

Comrade Napoleon.'

Build critical skills

How does Squealer calm the animals' fears about engaging in trade with humans? What point do you think Orwell is making about the trustworthiness of those in power?

Key quotation

'They had won, but they were weary and bleeding.'

Key quotation

'...it did seem to them after all that they had won a great victory.'

Build critical skills

Look back at old Major's speech in Chapter 1. How does Napoleon's behaviour contravene what old Major said?

Soon Frederick attacks Animal Farm, aided by a large group of armed men. Frederick's men use dynamite to blow up the windmill. In response, the enraged animals attack the men, driving them away, but they suffer heavy casualties in doing so; several animals are killed and Boxer sustains a serious injury. The animals feel dejected, but their faith is somewhat restored after a patriotic flag-raising ceremony. The Battle of the Windmill in the novel represents the Battle of Stalingrad, a turning point for Russia, when the Russians drove the invading German army out of Russia, though suffering huge casualties in the process.

A few days later, the pigs discover a crate of whisky in the farmhouse cellar and that night the animals hear singing and commotion and spot Napoleon wearing Mr Jones's old bowler hat. The next morning the pigs look bleary-eyed and sick, and Squealer emerges to tell the others that Comrade Napoleon is dying. A rumour that Snowball has poisoned him circulates, but by evening Napoleon has recovered.

The next night, some of the animals are woken by a noise that turns out to be Squealer, who has fallen off a ladder. Nearby are an overturned paint pot and a paint brush. Only Benjamin understands, but he says nothing. A few days later, the animals discover that the Seventh Commandment now reads, 'No animal shall drink alcohol *to excess*', but once again they blame their memories for remembering the commandment wrongly. In this chapter, Orwell shows the way in which the pigs' breaking of rules signifies the continuing loss of the ideals of Animalism.

Chapter 9

Life is hard, with rations reduced again in December for all animals, except the pigs and dogs, although Squealer explains this away.

Talk of animals retiring circulates, although none has. Boxer's twelfth birthday – the age of retirement for horses – is approaching and his hoof, which was injured in the battle, is giving him trouble. Both Clover and Benjamin tell him to work less hard but he does not listen. His only goal is to see the windmill off to a good start before he retires. He looks forward to a comfortable life in the pasture as a reward for his lifetime of hard work.

When four sows give birth to 31 piebald piglets, Napoleon is assumed to be the father and he commands that a schoolroom be built for their education. The extra mouths that need feeding place an even greater strain on the farm's limited resources.

Key quotation

'Squealer always spoke of it as a "readjustment", never as a "reduction"'

Key quotation

'in fact no animal had ever actually retired.'

Build critical skills

How does this chapter show the ways the pigs are being treated as privileged members of the farm? What do you think Orwell is saying about the link between power and privilege?

Stocks run low and rations reduce again in February. Trade increases. Napoleon begins ordering events called 'Spontaneous Demonstrations', where the animals march around the farm, listen to speeches and take pride in the glory of Animal Farm. When a few animals complain about the wasted time and cold this entails, the sheep, who love these Demonstrations, drown them out with bleats of 'Four legs good, two legs bad!'

In April, Animal Farm becomes a republic and Napoleon, the sole candidate for leadership, becomes President in a unanimous vote. The same day, documents are 'discovered' that reveal Snowball's complicity with Jones at the Battle of the Cowshed. It is now said that Snowball fought openly with Jones and cried 'Long live Humanity!', and that his injuries were caused by Napoleon's teeth. Because the battle occurred so long ago, the animals accept this new story.

In the middle of the summer, Moses the raven returns to the farm and begins to spread stories about Sugarcandy Mountain.

The way in which propaganda is used is emphasised here through Squealer, and Orwell makes clever use of Moses in this chapter to signify the way in which the pigs openly condemn his tales but use them to pacify the animals. This represents the way in which Stalin initially persecuted the Church, but did a complete U-turn towards religious tolerance when he needed to use it to support his failing power base against the Nazis of Germany.

The animals continue to work like slaves, rebuilding the windmill and erecting the new schoolroom. Even though his hoof has healed and he continues to work hard, Boxer's appearance changes – his hide is less shiny and his haunches are shrunken. One day, Boxer collapses while pulling stone for the windmill. The other animals rush to tell Squealer, while Benjamin and Clover stay by his side.

Squealer announces that Napoleon has arranged for Boxer to be treated in Willingdon at a human hospital to recuperate. When the van arrives a few days later, however, Benjamin reads the writing on the side and announces that Boxer is being sent to a glue maker to be slaughtered. The animals panic and start to call out to Boxer to escape. Then they hear him kicking feebly inside the van, but he is unable to get out.

Three days later, Squealer announces that Boxer has died in hospital. Claiming to have been at Boxer's side when he died, he talks of how moved he was and says that Boxer died praising the glories of Animal Farm. Squealer condemns the false rumours that Boxer was taken to a glue factory, and allays the animals' fears by telling them that the hospital had bought the van from a glue maker and had failed to paint over the van's lettering. The animals are relieved at this, and they feel completely placated when Napoleon gives a speech in praise of Boxer on the following Sunday.

Key quotation

'…and at the head of all marched Napoleon's black cockerel.'

Key quotation

'There lies Sugarcandy Mountain, that happy country where we poor animals shall rest for ever from our labours!'

Build critical skills

Why do you think that, although the pigs officially condemn these stories, they allow Moses to live on the farm without requiring him to work and give him beer?

Key quotation

'Boxer has fallen! He is lying on his side and can't get up!'

Key quotation

"Fools! Fools!" shouted Benjamin … "They are taking Boxer to the knacker's!"

Boxer's death and the farm's status changing to a republic with Napoleon as president is significant, as both these incidents signal a complete betrayal of its ideals.

Shortly afterwards, the farmhouse receives a delivery from the grocer and sounds of partying erupt from within. It becomes apparent that the pigs have found the money to buy another crate of whisky – though no one knows where they have acquired that money.

Chapter 10

Years pass and many animals age and die. Only Clover, Benjamin, Moses and a few pigs recall the days before the Rebellion. The farm is now organised and prosperous, with two additional fields having been bought from Pilkington. The windmill has been completed but is not used for generating electricity. Instead, corn is milled, providing the farm with much profit. Another windmill is being built but the luxuries Snowball talked of are denounced by Napoleon, who says Animalism is about hard work and frugal living.

While the farm seems to have grown richer, only the pigs and dogs live comfortably. Squealer explains that the pigs and dogs do important work – filling out forms and carrying out administrative tasks. Mostly, the other animals accept this explanation and their lives continue as before. Despite the hardships they endure, they never lose their sense of pride in Animal Farm. They still believe passionately in the goals of the Rebellion – in a world free from human tyranny, where all animals are equal.

One day, Squealer leads the sheep off to a remote spot to teach them a new song. Shortly afterwards, when the animals have just finished their day's work, they hear the horrified neighing of Clover, who summons the others to the yard. There, they find Squealer walking on his hind legs. Several other pigs follow suit before Napoleon emerges from the farmhouse, walking on his hind legs and carrying a whip.

GRADE BOOSTER

If you are asked about key plot points then showing that you understand this is a significant point in the novel may boost your marks. The whip is a symbol of tyranny and of Man. It is one of the instruments destroyed in Chapter 2, its destruction causing the animals to 'caper with joy'. So Napoleon carrying a whip is a direct contradiction of the foundations of the Rebellion and an indication of the novel's cyclical structure.

Before the other animals have a chance to vocalise their thoughts, the sheep begin to endlessly chant, 'Four legs good, two legs *better*!'

Clover asks Benjamin to read the writing on the barn wall where the Seven Commandments were originally inscribed, believing it to look different. When he does, he reads the one commandment that remains:

'ALL ANIMALS ARE EQUAL BUT SOME ANIMALS ARE MORE EQUAL THAN OTHERS.'

A week later, the pigs invite the neighbouring farmers over to inspect Animal Farm. The farmers praise the pigs and express admiration for what they see. Later, the pigs and humans mingle in the farmhouse. The other animals, led by Clover, watch through a window as Pilkington and Napoleon toast each other. Pilkington states that the mistrust and misunderstandings of the past are over. He shows admiration for the way the pigs have managed to make Animal Farm's animals work harder and on less food than any other group of farm animals in the county and he says that he looks forward to introducing these advances on his own farm.

He declares that the farmers share a problem with the pigs: 'If you have your lower animals to contend with,' he says, 'we have our lower classes!' Napoleon responds by reassuring his human guests that the pigs never wanted anything other than to conduct business peacefully with their human neighbours, rather than 'stir up rebellion'. He explains that the pigs now own the farm and that animals on Animal Farm will no longer address one another as 'comrade', or pay homage to old Major; nor will they salute a flag with a horn and hoof upon it. All of these customs have been changed recently by decree, he assures the men. Napoleon even announces that Animal Farm will from now on be known as Manor Farm, which is, he says, its 'correct and original name'.

The pigs and farmers return to their card game and the other animals creep away from the window. Soon, however, the sounds of a quarrel draw the animals back. Napoleon and Pilkington have both played the ace of spades; each accuses the other of cheating. As the animals watch through the window, they realise with horror that they can no longer distinguish between the pigs and the human beings.

With his last sentence, Orwell suggests the lost hopes and ideals of the long-forgotten Rebellion. He seems to be suggesting that all rebellions are doomed to fail and end with a totalitarian regime exploiting its citizens.

Key quotation

'already it was impossible to say which was which.'

Build critical skills

Orwell said of the novel that it was 'primarily a satire on the Russian Revolution' but he meant it to be more far-reaching and to relate to any revolution that was 'violent and conspiratorial' and 'led by unconsciously power-hungry people'. He suggested that this sort of revolution could succeed only with a change of leaders. How does Orwell present the violence of regime change in the novel?

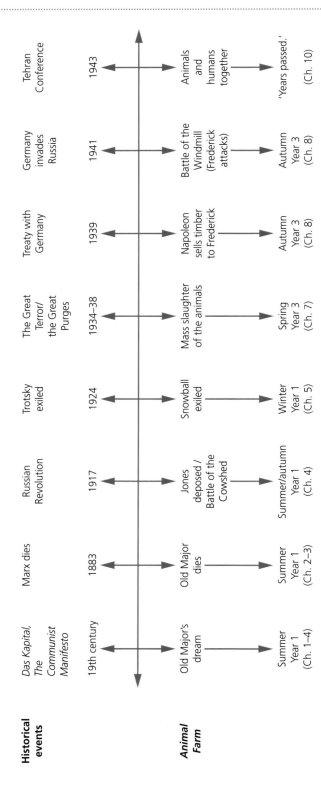

Historical events	*Das Kapital, The Communist Manifesto*	Marx dies	Russian Revolution	Trotsky exiled	The Great Terror/ the Great Purges	Treaty with Germany	Germany invades Russia	Tehran Conference
	19th century	1883	1917	1924	1934–38	1939	1941	1943
Animal Farm	Old Major's dream	Old Major dies	Jones deposed / Battle of the Cowshed	Snowball exiled	Mass slaughter of the animals	Napoleon sells timber to Frederick	Battle of the Windmill (Frederick attacks)	Animals and humans together
	Summer Year 1 (Ch. 1–4)	Summer Year 1 (Ch. 2–3)	Summer/autumn Year 1 (Ch. 4)	Winter Year 1 (Ch. 5)	Spring Year 3 (Ch. 7)	Autumn Year 3 (Ch. 8)	Autumn Year 3 (Ch. 8)	'Years passed.' (Ch. 10)

▲ Timeline of events

Structure

The most significant aspect of the novel's structure is its circular nature. The novel starts with Manor Farm and ends with Manor Farm, the ideals of Animal Farm having been totally destroyed. The novel starts with the animals being enslaved by a cruel master and ends with the animals being enslaved by a cruel master. Note that Mr Jones is a heavy drinker and Napoleon and the rest of the pigs are also heavy drinkers.

Orwell achieves this circular structure in several different ways:

1 The name of the farm. It starts out with the name Manor Farm; the animals change it to Animal Farm, but at the end of the novel Napoleon announces that it will be changed back to Manor Farm.

2 By changing the Seven Commandments, the pigs gradually become more and more like their former human masters. By the end of the novel the pigs are acting exactly as Jones and his men did before the Rebellion – carrying whips, wearing clothes, reading newspapers, sleeping in the farmhouse, drinking alcohol and generally behaving like humans in all aspects of their lives.

3 The most telling moment is at the very end of the novel when the rest of the animals look into the farmhouse and are unable to distinguish between pigs and humans. The humans have become pigs and the pigs have become human: nothing has changed for the rest of the animals.

The next page has a visual representation of this 'full circle' structure of *Animal Farm*.

This circular nature of the novel is essential in conveying Orwell's message. On one level he is showing us that the Russian Revolution failed in improving the lives of its people, as the new rulers (the Communist Party under Stalin) were just as bad as, or worse than, the old regime (under Tsar Nicholas II). Orwell also appears to be saying that unless the people are very vigilant, all revolutions will fail and people's lives will not be improved.

> ### Build critical skills
>
> Does the fact that the pigs and the humans look the same at the end of the novel mean Orwell is saying that greed and a lust for power are basic animal instincts in Mankind, which thus makes the creation of a Utopian society an impossibility?

> ### Key quotation
>
> *'The creatures outside looked from pig to man, and from man to pig, and from pig to man again; but it was impossible to say which was which.'*

> ### Build critical skills
>
> Give examples of Orwell showing that Mr Jones and Napoleon are similar in their attitude to alcohol.

> ### GRADE BOOSTER
>
> Why do you think Orwell called the farm 'Manor Farm'? Think about the phrase 'Lord of the Manor'. How does this relate to both Mr Jones and Napoleon?

> ### Key quotation
>
> *'He carried a whip in his trotter.'*

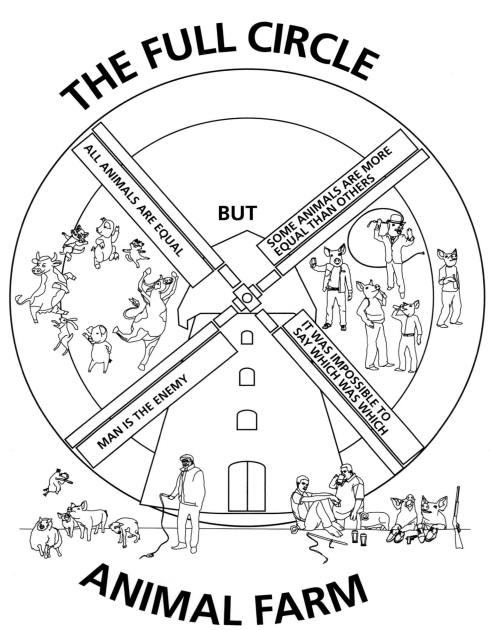

The full circle

GRADE BOOSTER

Being able to see the similarities of the opening and the ending of the novel, and hence its circular structure, demonstrates that you are aware of Orwell consciously crafting the novel to help in getting his message across to the reader. This will help you gain the higher levels.

GRADE FOCUS

Grade 5

To achieve a Grade 5 students will show a clear and detailed understanding of the whole text and of the effects created by its structure.

Grade 8

To achieve a Grade 8, students' responses will display a comprehensive understanding of explicit and implicit meanings in the text as a whole and will examine and evaluate in detail the writer's use of structure.

REVIEW YOUR LEARNING

(Answers are given on p. 102.)

1 What was the original name of Animal Farm?
2 What name is given to the political system developed from old Major's ideas?
3 What is the maxim taken up by the sheep?
4 Name the two neighbouring farms and their owners.
5 Who won the debate over the building of the windmill?
6 How is the Fourth Commandment broken?
7 How does Napoleon trick Whymper?
8 How are the Third and Fifth Commandments broken?
9 What do the pigs buy with the proceeds from selling Boxer?
10 What is the one commandment that replaces the Seven Commandments?
11 What is the most significant aspect of the novel's structure?

Characterisation

Target your thinking

- What role does each character play? (**AO1**, **AO2**)
- How does Orwell present the characters to us? (**AO2**)
- What evidence is there to help us form our opinion about each character? (**AO1**, **AO2**)
- What are the relationships between characters? (**AO1**)

Characters in a novel are revealed to us through a combination of techniques:

- by the author's direct description
- by what characters say and how they say it
- by what characters think and do
- by what others say and think about them
- by what they represent or symbolise (this is particularly important in *Animal Farm*).

GRADE BOOSTER

Remember that the characters in the novel have been created by a writer and that your focus needs to be on the ways in which the writer has presented the characters to the reader. If the words 'Orwell' or 'the writer' don't appear several times in your answer, you are probably not answering the question and you are unlikely to achieve high marks.

In *Animal Farm* Orwell uses characters to explore political and moral issues by means of a fable. Although they are seen to speak, behave and think like humans, they still retain their stereotypical animal image. In this way, they can be said to be anthropomorphic.

GRADE BOOSTER

Being able to write with confidence about characters and to make insightful comments may help you gain higher grades. Knowing what or who characters represent and how the language is used to describe them is a sign of a higher-level candidate.

Old Major (Willingdon Beauty)

Orwell describes old Major as a 'majestic-looking pig' with a 'benevolent appearance', suggesting his status among the other animals as revered and respected. In his dream of rebellion, old Major shows himself to be an ambitious character who is vehement about the commitment necessary for the rebellion.

He is presented as a powerful, persuasive speaker with a gift for rhetoric. For example, old Major's speech in the opening chapter inspires the animals to believe in a 'golden future time' when animals will be free. He speaks eloquently about his hopes for the future.

The speech is a strong call to action through which Orwell shows how Major uses a number of persuasive devices, including rhetorical questions, personal pronouns and emotive language. Words like 'miserable' and 'cruel' emphasise the sad plight of the animals, while his list of animals suggests that no one can escape this 'horror', as he calls it. He also uses alliteration in his rhetorical question when he asks, 'Is it not crystal clear then, comrades, that all the evils of this life of ours spring from the tyranny of human beings?' By describing humans as tyrants and using the possessive adjective 'ours', old Major depicts animals as victims united against Man. Orwell also highlights Major's effective use of the device of contrast when he refers to 'night and day, body and soul', suggesting the way that animals must dedicate themselves to overthrowing humans. His use of exclamations, assertions and imperatives makes old Major's message clear – that the animals must 'pass on this message' of rebellion so that they are ultimately 'victorious'.

Old Major is optimistic in his hopes for the future and is enthusiastic about the Rebellion and all it promises. It is evident that he is an intelligent and perceptive animal as he is able to assess the state of England at the time.

He seeks to pass on his wisdom before he dies, telling the animals of his dream and teaching them the song 'Beasts of England'. He urges the animals to remember their duty of 'enmity towards Man and all his ways'. He can be seen to represent Karl Marx and Friedrich Engels in particular, but can also be seen as any visionary and inspirational political thinker.

Marx was a German philosopher who believed that capitalists exploited the workers/proletariat in the same way that the humans are described as exploiting the animals in old Major's speech. Marx worked with Engels to create the *Communist Manifesto* in 1848, in which he called for workers to unite against their chains and to revolt against the capitalists, in the same way that old Major calls on the animals to rebel.

Build critical skills

Read again the description of old Major in Chapter 1. How does Orwell suggest the esteem with which the other animals view him?

Key quotation

'And remember, comrades, your resolution must never falter.'

Key quotation

'No animal in England is free. The life of an animal is misery and slavery: that is the plain truth.'

Napoleon

The name Napoleon is known all over the world because of the famous nineteenth-century French leader Napoleon Bonaparte, whose name became synonymous with tyranny. In the novel Napoleon proves himself to be one of the leading pigs, and later the most dominant pig on the farm. He is presented as a power-hungry pig whose ruthlessness causes the exile of Snowball and who uses others to gain power for himself.

Orwell uses the character of Napoleon to represent Stalin, a ruthless dictator who ruled Russia with iron force. Just as Stalin did to the Russian people, Napoleon uses clever tactics to gain and maintain control over the animals. He uses food as both a reward and a punishment — in Chapter 2, when the animals are rewarded after the Rebellion, and in Chapter 6, when he uses the threat of half rations to force the animals to work on a Sunday. Orwell contrasts him with Snowball in his ability to canvass support from others and it is clear that he is ruthless when he removes the puppies, only for them to later appear as his trained assassins.

He uses **duplicity** and cunning to maintain power. He increases the workload of the animals while decreasing their food rations (yet uses Squealer to suggest that this is not the case) and he insists that Sunday work is 'strictly voluntary'.

Napoleon's absence from the Battle of the Cowshed may suggest his cowardice, but Orwell tries to be fair. When he found out that Stalin had stayed in Moscow during the German Army's advance in World War II, Orwell instructed his publisher to change the text in Chapter 8. Instead of 'all the animals, *including* [my italics] Napoleon, flung themselves flat on their bellies', he asked that the text be changed to 'all the animals, *except* Napoleon...')

Orwell presents Napoleon's ruthless desire to maintain power when Napoleon starves the hens until they submit to his will and are forced to surrender their eggs, and when he slaughters animals in Chapter 7. Readers may well be shocked and repelled by this horrific display of brutality.

This, along with sending Boxer to his death and enjoying the crate of whisky acquired with the proceeds of his sale, indicates how Orwell presents the cruel and tyrannical nature of Napoleon in the strongest possible terms.

His selfishness is seen early on when it is inferred that he drank the milk in Chapter 2, thus breaking the most important of the commandments (that of the equality of all animals), almost immediately after the Rebellion. This selfishness increases as Napoleon distances himself from the other animals, appearing only occasionally and then with dogs around him and announced by a cockerel. He has the poem written by

Duplicity: deceitfulness, deception or double-dealing.

Build critical skills

Napoleon is described in Chapter 2 as 'fierce-looking' and as having a 'reputation for getting his own way'. How does this suggest what is to follow?

Key quotation

'...there was a pile of corpses lying before Napoleon's feet and the air was heavy with the smell of blood, which had been unknown there since the expulsion of Jones.'

Minimus inscribed on the barn wall and confers upon himself the 'Order of the Green Banner', all of which show Orwell presenting his self-obsessed character.

Napoleon is presented as hypocritical, breaking all the rules set for the other animals. Despite forbidding the other pigs from eating sugar, he has it himself and he openly flouts the Seven Commandments, adopting the vices of humans and going against old Major's original tenets.

Like Stalin, whom he represents, Orwell presents Napoleon as an original revolutionary who betrays the ideals of the Rebellion, is corrupted by power and turns into a dictator. He is the perfect example of the 'power-hungry people' who Orwell suggests should not become leaders after a rebellion.

Snowball

Orwell uses Snowball to represent Trotsky, who fought hard to ensure the success of the Russian Revolution. Trotsky believed in the ideals upon which the revolution was fought and he sought to improve life for the Russian people. So, too, Snowball seeks to improve the ways in which the animals work.

In Chapter 2, Orwell uses the words 'vivacious' and 'inventive' to describe him, and to distinguish him from Napoleon. We see this lively and attractive side of his character in the novel in his enthusiastic and endless pursuit of improvements. Orwell contrasts Snowball and Napoleon by describing the latter as 'not much of a talker'. We are told that Snowball had studied the *Farmer and Stockbreeder* and 'was full of plans for innovations and improvements'.

Orwell presents Snowball as being, like Trotsky, an intelligent intellectual who organises the animals into committees and seeks to educate the illiterate masses. He is the one to explain to the animals the reason behind the flag's symbols of hoof and horn and he simplifies the Seven Commandments for the less intelligent animals to 'Four legs good, two legs bad'.

His intelligence and foresight are seen when, having studied books about the battle campaigns of Julius Caesar, he organises the animals for battle and leads them in an ambush on the humans in the Battle of the Cowshed. Here, too, we see his courage as he suffers a wound and is awarded 'Animal Hero, First Class'.

He is the one to suggest and plan building a windmill to produce electricity and improve life for the animals. Orwell really shows Snowball's eloquence (which is first described in Chapter 2 when we are told that 'he was quicker in speech' than Napoleon) in his speech about the windmill and his vision of a farm run with electrical machinery.

Key quotation

'He took his meals alone, with two dogs to wait upon him, and always ate from the Crown Derby dinner service…'

Key quotation

Snowball: 'Let us make it a point of honour to get in the harvest more quickly than Jones and his men could do.'

Key quotation

'Without halting for an instant Snowball flung his fifteen stone against Jones's legs.'

As Trotsky was the natural successor to Lenin (Russia's first leader), Snowball is a natural leader able to inspire the animals with his ambitions for the farm and his eloquence. This is why he poses such a threat to Napoleon.

Just as in 1927 Stalin exiled Trotsky, Napoleon has his dogs chase Snowball off the farm. Snowball is then presented as Napoleon's scapegoat for all that goes wrong on the farm. Readers will respond to the injustice as he is slandered, said to have been 'in league with Jones from the very start' and later to have 'never … received the order of "Animal Hero, First Class".'

He becomes a tool used by Napoleon and the other pigs to create fear and maintain control over the other animals. Although Orwell creates great sympathy for Snowball, he should not be seen as perfect: Snowball is quite willing to accept the privileges the pigs give themselves.

Squealer

Squealer is used by Napoleon as the voice of propaganda. Where the pigeons initially spread the word of Animalism to other farms, Squealer spreads the word of the new regime under Napoleon.

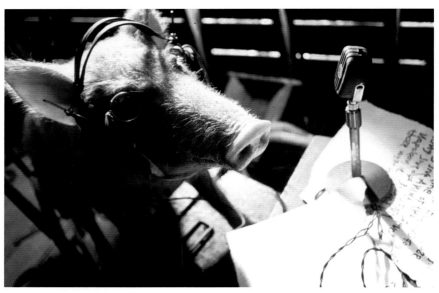

▲ Squealer makes a broadcast in the 1999 film

Orwell uses him to show the way in which politicians manipulate language and also rewrite history. Just as Joseph Stalin was able to control the press, Napoleon is able through Squealer to control what information is provided and how it is delivered.

In Chapter 2, Orwell describes Squealer as 'a small fat pig', suggesting self-indulgence as well as creating a slightly ridiculous figure. He is also described as a 'brilliant talker' who 'could turn black into white', suggesting his ability to persuade others of the truth of something which is clearly not true. This skill is seen on numerous occasions as conditions on the farm deteriorate and as the pigs assume more and more control. Today, we might refer to him as a 'spin doctor', someone who twists facts for their own political ends.

Orwell's name for Squealer fits him well in that it refers both to his 'shrill voice', which defines him, and to his ability to betray his fellow animals. His 'nimble movements' and 'way of skipping from side to side and whisking his tail' suggest a slippery, evasive character who is hard to pin down. Squealer's deceitfulness is apparent in his actions: painting over the commandments as clearly seen in Chapter 8, claiming to have visited Boxer at his deathbed and lying about old Major's tenets.

Squealer causes the animals to question their memories: through using his persuasive skills and the fear of the dogs that attend him, he is always able to, as Orwell writes, 'put the matter in its proper perspective'.

Squealer also has a threatening presence. Despite his apparent efforts to appease the animals, he is always attended by the dogs, who ensure that his message is accepted. This more menacing side to Squealer is seen when Boxer questions his version of the Battle of the Cowshed in Chapter 7, when he gives Boxer 'a very ugly look' – only for Boxer to be attacked by the dogs later in the chapter. It is also seen when Squealer informs the animals of the error they made in assuming Boxer was going to the knacker's yard in Chapter 9.

His defence of Napoleon's actions, describing his taking on the role of leader as a 'sacrifice' and indicating that everything that Napoleon does is for the benefit of all, shows his loyalty to Napoleon. Squealer's lack of conscience is evident in the way in which he blatantly lies time and again. This, and his unwavering loyalty to Napoleon, make him the perfect propagandist for the tyrannical dictator Napoleon.

Boxer

Boxer is one of the cart-horses on the farm and as such he represents the working classes, or proletariat. He is described from the start as being 'as strong as any two horses put together'. After the Rebellion, Boxer's commitment to the cause increases, as does his strength, with Orwell stating that he 'seemed more like three horses than one' and describing him as having strength equal to all the other animals put together.

This strength is put to great use both at harvest time and in the building of the windmill, where it is Boxer alone who is able to drag boulders to the top of the quarry. He is essential to the success of the farm.

> **Key quotation**
>
> *'Are you certain that this is not something you have dreamed, comrades?'*

> **Key quotation**
>
> *'Squealer spoke so persuasively, and the three dogs who happened to be with him growled so threateningly, that they accepted his explanation without further questions.'*

> **Build critical skills**
>
> 'Here Squealer's demeanour suddenly changed. He fell silent for a moment, and his little eyes darted suspicious glances from side to side before he proceeded.' How does Orwell use detail in this description to suggest that Squealer is not to be trusted?

> **Key quotation**
>
> *'...there were days when the entire work of the farm seemed to rest upon his mighty shoulders.'*

His hard-working nature is epitomised by his personal motto of 'I will work harder' and by the fact that he arranges with the cockerels for them to wake him earlier than the others. His dedication to duty and commitment to the farm are evident in his hard work and consistent efforts, and it is this dedication and hard work that gain him the admiration of his fellow animals.

Despite his physical strength, Boxer lacks intelligence and is therefore unable to learn his alphabet beyond the letter D, although he practises these letters religiously every day to remind himself of them.

When he collapses, it is natural for many of the animals to rush to the knoll to see what has happened. Boxer's selflessness is markedly apparent at this moment, when he thinks of the farm rather than of himself in saying that the others should be able to finish the windmill without him. Orwell uses his bravery and naivety to create both admiration and pity in the reader. His constant dedication to duty makes his cruel treatment at the hands of the pigs all the more callous and Orwell sharply contrasts his demeanour with theirs.

Boxer's inability to see fault in the pigs contributes to his second motto of 'Napoleon is always right' and to his belief that Napoleon's mass execution of the animals must be due to some fault in the animals themselves. It is this very loyalty and trusting nature, however, that makes it easy for the pigs to exploit and abuse him, ultimately selling him to the knacker's yard once he no longer has the strength to move, and purchasing a crate of whisky with the proceeds.

Orwell uses Boxer as an example of the proletariat, and in particular of a hard-working citizen who is exploited by authority. Boxer eventually pays for blindly supporting a cause with his life.

Despite appearing to honour Boxer at the memorial banquet dedicated to him, Napoleon and the other pigs show their utter contempt for him and the working classes he represents by drinking whisky purchased from his sale to the knackers, creating a nauseating effect for the reader.

Benjamin

Benjamin the donkey is described in Chapter 1 as 'the oldest animal on the farm and the worst tempered'. He is a cynic who does not believe that anything will change on the farm. After the Rebellion he remains much the same as he always was, 'never shirking and never volunteering for extra work either'.

His depiction as a donkey is quite significant in that he is neither quite a horse (the proletariat) nor a leader like the pigs, despite his intellect being equal to theirs. Donkeys typically live long lives and are often seen as long-suffering.

Benjamin is a complex character. Some have suggested that he represents the older population of Russia, or that he represents the **Menshevik** intelligentsia – the intelligent section of the minority moderate Russian political party.

Menshevik: minority political group that expressed more moderate views than the Bolsheviks.

Regardless of which sector of Russian society Benjamin represents, it could be argued that Orwell presents him as a symbol of intelligence, in that during the times of revolution and its aftermath he is aware of what is going on but does nothing about it. His inaction may be explained away as he says, that 'Donkeys live a long time.'

He refuses to express an opinion on the Rebellion or on whether life will be better after it, offering instead cryptic responses. For the most part, Orwell uses him to represent those sceptics both within and outside of Russia who believed that communism would not help the Russian people, but who did not criticise it enough to risk their lives.

Benjamin's intelligence is apparent in that he 'could read as well as any pig', although he chooses not to exercise this skill. Later, in Chapter 8, he is the only animal to fully comprehend what Snowball is doing with the paint, but again he chooses to say nothing. The only time he breaks this rule is when he reads what is written on the van that takes Boxer away. His loyalty to Boxer is exemplified towards the end of the novel: Benjamin's commitment is evident in the way he sits with Boxer while he is ill, making him a more sympathetic character for the reader.

Key quotation

'...*without openly admitting it, he was devoted to Boxer...*'

Build critical skills

What do you think Orwell might have wished us to think to be the reasons behind Benjamin's lack of involvement in the Rebellion and its aftermath?

In Chapter 10, when Clover asks Benjamin to read what is written on the barn wall, he does so but by this time it is too late – the pigs have well and truly taken over the farm and cannot be distinguished from the men with whom they are drinking.

The name Benjamin means 'son of my right hand' or 'son of right'. This could support the argument that Orwell intended Benjamin to be seen as a realist. Another view is that Benjamin's cynicism reflects Orwell's own views of a Western world eventually being taken over by totalitarian governments. Certainly, Benjamin's views that nothing will ever be 'much better or much worse' but will go on as it always has, turn out to be right in the world of the novel.

Mollie

Orwell presents Mollie as a 'pretty white mare' who pulls Jones's trap. She represents the White Russians who under tsarist rule had a privileged life, in her case represented by sugar and ribbons.

She is said to ask the 'stupidest questions' and is shown to have early reservations about life without Jones when she wants to keep her ribbons and sugar. Orwell states that she 'agreed but did not sound very convinced'. Here he is giving an indication of things to come when

Mollie later defects to a neighbouring farm. Orwell states that 'she strolls blithely into the yard, flirting her tail' when Clover confronts her about her being seen with one of Pilkington's men; this implies she has a superficial nature and will not heed Clover. When she is accused she lies and begins to 'prance about and paw the ground' — again suggesting that she cannot face up to her shameful behaviour. She is later seen allowing 'a fat red-faced man ... who looked like a publican' to stroke her nose and feed her sugar. Orwell is suggesting that she is fickle and likes her luxuries. Sugar is a man-made refined substance that is not good for horses and which is used here to suggest her collusion with the enemy.

She is vain, looking at herself in the mirror in the farmhouse and learning only those letters that spell her name. Orwell presents her as a shirker who avoids work whenever possible.

At the Battle of the Cowshed, she is found hiding in her stall. This and her constant shirking of work portray Mollie as a lazy and non-committed member of the farm. Her desertion to a neighbouring farm represents those Russians who defected to the West in search of a better life.

Clover

Clover is depicted as a 'stout motherly mare'. Orwell establishes her caring nature early on in the novel when a brood of motherless ducklings files into the barn and she creates a wall with her great foreleg behind which the ducklings nestle. We discover that she has lost four of her foals (they have been sold) and this may explain her motherly tendencies as well as creating sympathy for her. Indeed, it is around her that the other animals huddle when several animals are killed in Chapter 7.

Clover's constant, kind and caring nature is seen throughout the novel and in particular in her loyalty to Boxer, whom she warns not to overstrain himself and whom she tends to when he collapses.

Orwell shows that she has some intelligence as she is able to learn the whole alphabet, although she cannot read full words. It is this that allows her to recognise the change on the barn wall in Chapter 10 that Benjamin reads for her.

Like Boxer, she is said never to lose heart, firmly believing in the ideals of the Rebellion. Following the purges of Chapter 7, however, Orwell allows us a brief insight into her thoughts, as her 'eyes filled with tears'. He uses her to voice the thoughts of the other animals who, like her, lack the words to express themselves (see the key quotation in the margin).

Despite her disappointment about what is actually happening on the farm, she resolves to work hard and remain faithful, for there is 'no thought of rebellion or disobedience in her mind'. She decides to sing 'Beasts of England' as an expression of her belief in the ideals of

Key quotation

Clover's thoughts: 'If she herself had had any picture of the future, it had been of a society of animals set free from hunger and the whip, all equal, each working according to his capacity'

Animalism. Even this is short-lived when Squealer bans the song, once again reinforcing her inability to express herself.

Clover, like Benjamin, is one of the few animals who live to the end of the novel. She remembers the Rebellion and the foundations upon which Animal Farm was built. This, then, explains the horror with which she greets the sight of Squealer on his hind legs.

Orwell makes Clover a significant character for it is often through her eyes that he shows us the ideals of Animalism eroding. It is she who leads the other animals to the window in the last chapter, where they witness the final destruction of all the principles upon which the Rebellion had been built.

The pigs

Orwell depicts the pigs in the novel as the most intelligent of the animals. This is why they assume leadership. Orwell signals for us at the very start of the novel the higher status that the pigs will assume later, when they sit directly in front of the platform from which old Major delivers his speech in Chapter 1.

By Chapter 3, it is apparent that the pigs do not share the animals' workload. Instead they 'directed and supervised the others' and when they start to give themselves bigger rations, taking the apples and milk, this is a solitary point on which both Napoleon and Snowball agree.

Orwell uses the pigs to represent the revolutionaries corrupted by power, who enjoy their position at the top and as a result seek to maintain the status quo. As the novel progresses, we see the way in which the pigs take on the role formerly occupied by Jones.

▲ The pigs have become like humans

Key quotation

'The work of teaching and organising the others fell naturally upon the pigs, who were generally recognised as being the cleverest of the animals.'

Key quotation

'So it was agreed without further argument that the milk and the windfall apples (and also the main crop of apples when they ripened) should be reserved for the pigs alone.'

Key quotation

'Somehow it seemed as though the farm had grown richer without making the animals themselves any richer – except of course for the pigs and the dogs.'

The dogs

At the start of the novel, Orwell indicates the important role that the dogs will play when they are the first to enter the barn to hear old Major's speech. Their violence is also hinted at early on when they attack the rats in Chapter 1.

We are not fully aware of why Orwell has Napoleon remove the dogs' puppies in Chapter 3, until they reappear to chase Snowball off the farm. Thereafter, however, they play an important role in controlling the animals through fear, just as the Secret Police in Russia aided Stalin in his control over the masses. Control through fear and violence is a common factor in totalitarian regimes.

Their loyalty to Napoleon is apparent in that they attend him wherever he goes and sit by his bedside while he sleeps. Orwell's description of their wagging tails when in Napoleon's presence draws a comparison between Napoleon and Jones. The dogs are rewarded for this loyalty, enjoying a richer life than the other animals. They always accompany Squealer when he 'explains' the pigs' decisions, to ensure that there is no dissent from the other animals.

The sheep

Orwell presents the sheep as the most unintelligent sector of society. Snowball simplifies the commandments to the maxim of 'Four legs good, two legs bad' in order to help them understand Animalism, but they are easily manipulated by Napoleon, who succeeds in canvassing their support. Their constant bleating of 'Four legs good, two legs bad!' interrupts meetings and suggests their lack of understanding. Subsequently, when they drown out Snowball's speech, we see the damage such blind support can cause: they unknowingly stifle free speech.

Later, they are easily manipulated by Squealer when he teaches them the mantra of 'Four legs good, two legs *better*'. Orwell uses them to represent those members of society who are used as tools for a cause and are manipulated for politicians' own ends.

Mr Jones

Mr Jones's role is to represent the aristocracy and ruling class in Russia, in particular Tsar Nicholas II, who was shot in 1918. Mr Jones is portrayed as an uncaring man who neglects the farm and his animals, treating them cruelly and taking everything they produce. The opening sentence of the novel firmly establishes Mr Jones as a negligent figure, stating that he was 'too drunk' to tend to his duties properly.

The details provided by old Major suggest the tyranny with which Mr Jones rules the farm, his despicable attitude to the animals and the way in which he represents tsarism and capitalism. The animals under Jones's rule suffered a similar fate to that of the peasants in Russia under tsarist rule.

Jones is described as always having been a 'hard master', but Orwell does point out that he had been a 'capable farmer' and had only taken to drink as a result of losing money in a lawsuit. In the opening pages, however, Orwell provides a damning description of the mismanagement of the farm as Jones lounges about drinking and reading his paper. 'His men were idle and dishonest, the fields were full of weeds, the buildings wanted roofing, the hedges were neglected, and the animals were underfed.'

The sympathy he gains from his neighbouring farmers is false, as Orwell indicates that they secretly wish to gain from his misfortune.

Jones's attempts to regain the farm end in defeat and we are told that he has died 'in an inebriates' home in another part of the country'.

Orwell does not have Jones physically feature much in the novel but he is constantly presented as the enemy. Throughout the novel, he is used by the pigs as a symbol of fear for the animals; his mere mention ensures the pigs' control. After a rebellion, it is natural for a new regime to blame all wrongs on the previous rulers and to use the threat of them returning as a means of control.

> **Key quotation**
>
> *Old Major: 'He sets them to work, he gives back to them the bare minimum that will prevent them from starving, and the rest he keeps for himself.'*

Mr Pilkington

Pilkington is one of Animal Farm's neighbouring farmers. His farm, Foxwood, is described as 'large, neglected' and 'old-fashioned'. Orwell describes him as a gentleman farmer who spends most of his time fishing or hunting.

Like Frederick, Pilkington fears the Rebellion extending to other farms and so he spreads rumours of wickedness on Animal Farm. Initially an enemy, Napoleon later befriends him.

Pilkington represents Britain under Churchill. His presence at the celebrations with Napoleon and Frederick at the end of the novel symbolises Stalin and Churchill's alliance with Roosevelt at the Tehran Conference in 1943. The quarrel at the end indicates the Cold War that followed this time.

Mr Frederick

Frederick is another of Jones's neighbours. His farm, Pinchfield, is smaller but better kept than Pilkington's, and Orwell describes him as 'a tough, shrewd man'. He is initially depicted as a man who drives a hard bargain and is said to be 'perpetually involved in lawsuits'.

GRADE *FOCUS*

Grade 5

To achieve a Grade 5, students will demonstrate a clear understanding of how and why Orwell uses language, form and structure to create characters, supported by appropriate references to the text.

Grade 8

To achieve a Grade 8, students will examine and evaluate the ways that Orwell uses language, form and structure to create characters, supported by carefully chosen and well-integrated references to the text.

This prepares us for the complicated negotiations over timber that he conducts with Napoleon. The way he tricks Napoleon with the forged notes symbolises the way in which Russia was deceived by Germany under Hitler when, despite a non-aggression pact, Germany attacked Russia, causing much destruction.

In Chapter 10, Orwell uses Frederick to represent the USA under Roosevelt at the Tehran Conference, with the implied suggestion of the Cold War as a result of the quarrel at the end of the novel.

Moses

Moses is depicted by Orwell as Mr Jones's 'especial pet', a spy and tale-bearer. He represents organised religion and the state Church, placating the animals with tales of Sugarcandy Mountain, somewhere animals go after a life of misery – in other words, a representation of Heaven. Orwell uses him to reflect Marx's view of religion as an 'opiate of the masses' that promised a wonderful afterlife in an effort to make people accept the pain of their current lives. Thus, in doing so, religion prevented people from changing their lives for the better.

Moses is a useful ally to both Jones and the pigs as he promises the animals that all their sacrifices will be rewarded in Sugarcandy Mountain. By presenting Moses in this way Orwell may be suggesting that organised religion supports the power of the state and not the ordinary man.

REVIEW YOUR LEARNING

(Answers are given on pp. 102–103.)

1. In what different ways can characters be revealed to us by a writer?
2. Identify three adjectives that Orwell uses to describe Napoleon and three to describe Snowball. Explain what these adjectives imply about these two characters.
3. Which animals represent the most stupid sector of society?
4. Which character represents organised religion?
5. List the characters whom Orwell has used to represent the following: Marx, Stalin, Trotsky, those who defected to the West, the Secret Police.

Themes

Target your thinking

- What are themes and why are they important in a novel? (**AO1**, **AO3**)
- What are the main themes of *Animal Farm*? (**AO1**, **AO3**)
- How does Orwell present his themes? (**AO1**, **AO2**, **AO3**)

The themes in a novel are an expression of the author's key ideas. While the plot or storyline tells us *what* happens in the novel, themes tell us *why*: repeatedly conveying the message(s) the author wants to give the readers that may make them reconsider their attitudes and even their behaviour.

Remember that in *Animal Farm* Orwell is creating the events in order to get his ideas across to the reader; and it is these ideas you should be writing about in your exam, not just the events themselves. To read *Animal Farm* as a simple children's 'fairy tale' is to entirely miss Orwell's purpose in writing the novel and won't get you any marks in the exam!

Although the main themes of *Animal Farm* can be said to be connected with the Russian Revolution, it is important to remember that the allegory is applicable to any totalitarian regime. Orwell's universal themes – warning of the failure of such revolutions to achieve their ideals and the abuse, corruption and tyranny that can result – make the novel still relevant today.

Orwell is not criticising socialist revolution in itself – after all, the animals' lives do initially improve, before the pigs begin to abuse their leadership. Orwell appears to endorse the principles behind the animals' revolution but attacks the tyranny and hypocrisy that inevitably follows. A key moment in the novel is in Chapter 7, when Clover attempts to understand the mass executions she has just witnessed. Orwell writes 'If

Build critical skills

Considering the fact that the other animals are so easily manipulated by the pigs, how far is Orwell's *Animal Farm* not so much warning us against the abuse of power as it is commenting on the inevitability of any revolution being replaced by an equally corrupt regime?

she could have spoken her thoughts...' This is the key point: the animals are incapable of articulating their thoughts and feelings and thus are easy prey to Squealer's lies and persuasive techniques.

There are several ways of categorising the themes of *Animal Farm* and in any interpretation of the novel there is bound to be some overlap. Here is a suggested list of how the main themes of *Animal Farm* might be grouped:

- idealism vs reality (utopia vs dystopia)
- greed and the corrupting influence of power
- violence and rebellion
- propaganda
- totalitarianism.

Idealism vs reality (utopia vs dystopia)

Old Major's initial ideas reveal the idealism of revolutionaries, which will contrast with the reality of subsequent events. This conflict between **utopia** and **dystopia** is central to an understanding of the novel. Orwell said that *Animal Farm* was founded on the basis of a utopian world – an ideal that old Major describes in his speech at the start of the novel and to which Orwell refers throughout the text.

The utopian world that is depicted is encapsulated in the song 'Beasts of England'. This serves as an anthem for the animals' cause and reminds us of 'The Red Flag', a famous socialist song, and of the 'Internationale', the international communist anthem. In 'Beasts of England' Orwell presents us with many positive words such as 'joyful tidings', 'golden future time', 'fruitful fields' and 'riches more than mind can picture', along with references to freedom. All of these phrases convey the idyllic image of a happy future full of prosperity and freedom to which the animals look forward. This ideal appears to become a reality in Chapter 2, straight after the Rebellion.

The symbolism of the animals waking at dawn the day after the Rebellion is clear, as it suggests a new beginning for them – a rebirth. This is emphasised when Orwell later writes, 'It was as though they had never seen these things before.' Words such as 'glorious' and 'clear morning light' indicate the purity of the utopian world that has come about as a result of the Rebellion. The repetition of the word 'theirs' suggests the importance of ownership and conveys the socialist ideals of freedom and collectivism. Orwell communicates the animals' absolute joy through words such as 'ecstasy', 'gambolled' and 'leaps of excitement', thus conveying the euphoria associated with freedom and ownership, which are again referred to when he repeats 'they could hardly believe that it was all their own'.

The placement of old Major's speech at the start of the novel ensures that readers are aware of the utopian world to which the animals aspire. By referring back to this speech throughout the novel, Orwell uses it as a benchmark against which we can judge events. This ensures that we are aware of the way in which this ideal is being corrupted.

Orwell makes evident the way in which the animals at first enjoy this ideal when he writes that 'Every mouthful of food was an acute positive pleasure, now that it was truly their own food, produced by themselves and for themselves.' By the end of the novel, despite the gradual deterioration in conditions and the obvious breaking of the commandments, the animals still hold on to this ideal, believing in it.

Orwell shows the way in which the masses are deluded into believing in an ideal, only to be exploited by those in power as this ideal is corrupted.

Orwell also shows that the way in which the ideal vision presented by old Major in Chapter 1 is altered is the same as the way in which the socialist ideal that he saw in Spain was lost. The first evidence of this is seen in Chapter 2 when the pigs are identified as the most clever, thus differentiating among the animals and going against the belief in equality. When Napoleon remains behind with the milk, only for it to disappear, we can see what the animals cannot, and we are therefore unsurprised to read of the pigs directing the others to work in Chapter 3. In Chapter 5, the animals are described as having 'worked like slaves' and their food is described as no more than in Jones's time. It is clear that the world is less of an ideal now for the animals than in Chapter 2, although Orwell ironically points out that 'they grudged no effort or sacrifice' because what they were doing was for 'the benefit of themselves … and not for a pack of idle thieving human beings'. He makes clear that the animals still believe in the ideal. When Napoleon announces he will engage in trade, however, Orwell draws our attention back to old Major's speech and refers to the animals' 'vague uneasiness'.

Greed and the corrupting influence of power

Another theme of the novel is greed and the corrupting influence of power. The pigs are the natural leaders and quickly become a privileged section of farm society. They immediately take advantage of this elitism, reserving the milk and apples, and later the barley, for themselves. Napoleon is able to use the greed of the other pigs and dogs to further his own ends in building up his power base. The subsequent changing of the Seven Commandments gives a more luxurious lifestyle to the pigs as well as reinforcing Napoleon's control, and the dogs' rations are never decreased ('readjusted', to use Squealer's word). Another device the pigs

Key quotation

'they woke at dawn … now they could hardly believe that it was all their own.'

Key quotation

'And yet the animals never gave up hope … They were still the only farm in the whole country – in all England! – owned and operated by animals.'

Key quotation

'They found it comforting to be reminded that … they were truly their own masters and that the work they did was for their own benefit.'

use to maintain power is their access to resources. Napoleon uses food to maintain control over the animals. He uses it as a reward in Chapter 2 and as a punishment in Chapter 6.

> **GRADE BOOSTER**
>
> Does the milk-taking incident show that power corrupts (and absolute power corrupts absolutely)? Or do you think Napoleon is already corrupt and that the power he gains simply enables him to display this corrupt/evil nature? Considering different interpretations of events like this is a great way to gain the highest levels.

Money is also a resource that allows the pigs to have power, for it is money that enables them to buy the necessary goods (oil, nails, string, dog biscuits) for the farm and whisky for themselves. When Napoleon sells the timber to Frederick, the animals are made to file past the money, which is presented on a china dish like food. Later, we see Napoleon state that he wants 'normal business relations with their neighbours', indicating the importance he places on trade as he recognises the power this gives him.

Violence and rebellion

Key quotation

'And so, almost before they knew what was happening, the Rebellion had been successfully carried through'

Although the ideas in old Major's dream had been discussed frequently by the animals, the actual Rebellion was unplanned and unexpected. The level of violence was quite low — one stunned farm boy, a wounded Snowball and one dead sheep (not even named).

This contrasts sharply with the extreme violence later in the novel, especially the false confessions and mass executions, which have their parallels in Russian history with the actual Russian Revolution (1917) and Stalin's show trials — the years of the 'Great Purge' in the 1930s (see pp. 12–13 in the 'Context' section).

Once the Rebellion has been successful, a power vacuum is created, which Napoleon fills by several means. One method is to use and exploit others. Thus the farm is an initial success because all (really most) of the animals work together for the common good. A clear example of this is gathering in the harvest 'in two days' less time than it had usually taken Jones and his men', while Napoleon, Snowball and Squealer work together to formulate the principles of Animalism. The Rebellion had inspired the animals, for example Boxer's great strength, and the pigs exploit this for their own ends: the rest of the animals do the hard work while the pigs gain the privileges.

Violence is used to initially wrest power from Farmer Jones and is necessary once again to create an all-powerful dictator. Snowball appears to be winning the election campaign with his eloquent speeches and plans for a windmill. Napoleon, however, has been preparing for this eventuality. We learn what is meant when he said 'he would make himself responsible for their [Jessie and Bluebell's puppies'] education'. Just as the Russian Revolution had produced an internal power struggle between Stalin and Trotsky, so it is in *Animal Farm* between Napoleon and Snowball. Snowball is driven off the farm by these fierce dogs and is lucky to escape with his life. (Trotsky was assassinated on Stalin's orders in Mexico in 1940.)

Of course there is no point in gaining power and becoming a dictator unless you can maintain your control over the population. Napoleon uses many tried-and-tested dictatorial techniques to keep and strengthen control over the animals as a greater level of fear and violence becomes needed to maintain and tighten his grip on Animal Farm. A constant threat to the animals is that if they don't agree with Squealer's explanations of Napoleon's actions, Farmer Jones will return. Towards the end of the novel most of the animals who knew Jones are dead; but the threat is still perceived as very real.

Fear and violence are mostly the preserve of the nine dogs Napoleon has reared since they were weaned. Note, however, that Jones also used fear and violence as a means of control: his gun 'always stood in a corner of his bedroom' and he shows scant regard for the safety of the animals when he fires into the darkness. His whip also becomes an important symbol of oppression. In Chapter 2 the animals 'capered with joy when they saw the whips going up in flames', but in the last chapter this symbol returns, as Napoleon emerges carrying 'a whip in his trotter'. The sight of this amazes and terrifies the animals.

Build critical skills

The dogs' inclination to violence is evident even in Chapter 1, when they attack the rats. Could this action have given Napoleon the idea of using dogs to control the animals once he gains power?

Build critical skills

'They [the dogs] kept close to Napoleon … they wagged their tails to him in the same way as the other dogs had been used to do to Mr Jones.' What is implied by this action and how does it foreshadow the end of the novel?

Build critical skills

Do you think that Napoleon was initially genuine in his belief in Animalism? Or was he using this ideology for his own ends from the beginning?

Key quotation

'Vote for Napoleon and the full manger'

'Vote for Snowball and the three-day week.'

Key quotation

'They dashed straight for Snowball, who only sprang from his place just in time to escape their snapping jaws'

Key quotation

'Surely none of you wished to see Jones back?'

Key quotation

'Though not yet full-grown, they were huge dogs, and as fierce-looking as wolves.'

Key quotation

'The three dogs who happened to be with him [Squealer] growled so threateningly, that they [the animals] accepted his explanation without further questions.'

Key quotation

'Once again, all rations were reduced, except those of the pigs and dogs.'

Key quotation

'When they had finished their confession, the dogs promptly tore their throats out'

Once the dogs have emerged to chase Snowball off the farm, they are an ever-present feature to ensure there is no dissent from the animals. When four young porkers voice their disapproval, the dogs 'let out deep, menacing growls' and the pigs 'fell silent'. They accompany Squealer whenever he explains Napoleon's orders, reinforcing Squealer's persuasiveness.

In the same way, Stalin's use of propaganda was reinforced by the presence of the Secret Police to stifle criticism. The dogs' effect on the rest of the animals is clear. After Snowball's expulsion by the dogs, the animals creep back to the barn 'silent and terrified'.

The dogs become part of an elite and privileged society and so remain loyal to Napoleon, carrying out his orders without question, such as ensuring no animal gives food to the striking hens so that nine starve to death before they give in.

The savagery of the dogs is best shown in the slaying of the four young porkers who earlier had voiced opposition to Napoleon. The dogs had 'tasted blood' and 'appeared to go quite mad'.

The mass confessions and executions that follow are all carried out by the dogs, who seem to relish the task. Only Boxer, with his great strength, is able to resist them.

GRADE BOOSTER

We are never given a reason for the dogs' attack on Boxer but when Squealer explains to the animals that Snowball has always been a traitor, Boxer is at first a 'little uneasy' and Squealer casts 'a very ugly look' at him since unquestioned obedience is demanded by Napoleon. Giving your own interpretation of events is a great way to gain the higher levels.

The true purpose of the false confessions and mass executions is twofold. It instils more fear into the animals by showing what will happen to any animal who voices dissent and so makes them less likely to question Napoleon's decisions. Secondly, it permanently eliminates any opposition.

Build critical skills

The dogs are unable to eliminate Boxer, who represents the working population, by force. Is Orwell saying that the people can never fully be controlled by a tyrant using force and that therefore there is hope for the future? Or is the fact that the dogs attack even Boxer, the most loyal follower of Napoleon, more evidence of the total evil of this regime? What do you think?

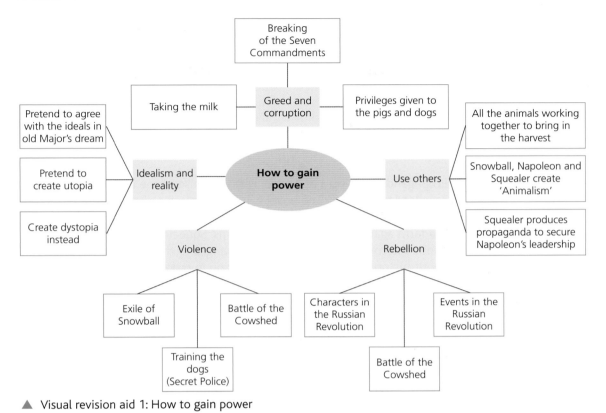

▲ Visual revision aid 1: How to gain power

Propaganda

Propaganda is an essential tool for any regime wanting to maintain its grip on the population. Squealer is the organ of propaganda on the farm. His first appearance in this role is in Chapter 3, when he explains away the pigs eating the apples and milk as being because they are 'brain-workers' and need to protect the farm from Mr Jones. Later he explains away Snowball's expulsion and rewrites history, stating that Napoleon was never really against the building of the windmill and that Snowball was Jones's secret agent all along.

Squealer's persuasive and dramatic speeches help Napoleon justify his actions and policies by whatever means seem necessary. He uses statistics to deceive the other animals, 'proving' that production of food had increased 'by 200 per cent, 300 per cent, or 500 per cent, as the case might be.' Because all the information that the animals get comes only from Squealer, they 'saw no reason to disbelieve him'.

Build critical skills

Note how Orwell satirically criticises Squealer's use of statistics when he writes 'All the same, there were days when they felt that they would sooner have had less figures and more food.' It is well known that statistics can be used to prove almost anything! A popular saying has it that there are three kinds of falsehood: lies, damned lies and statistics. What other examples can you find of Orwell's use of satire to criticise the pigs' regime?

Propaganda flourishes at Animal Farm because of the lies and deception practised by the pigs. The novel is full of examples of deception being used as a tool both to maintain control over the animals and to protect the farm against the neighbouring farms. Squealer lies to the animals about the commandments and the changes to the ideals, about Snowball, about history and about farm production in order to delude them into thinking they are well off.

Napoleon and (unwittingly) the other animals conspire in deceiving the humans into believing food is plentiful on Animal Farm when Napoleon shows Whymper around the farm in Chapter 7.

In Chapter 10, Orwell shows the extent of the lies and deception on the farm when Napoleon betrays all the ideals of the Rebellion. The pigs are said now to own the farm, the term 'comrades' is to be dropped and the name Manor Farm is to be reinstated. Orwell's experience had led him to believe that in a time of universal deceit, telling the truth was a revolutionary act.

The use of simple slogans and mottos is an important propaganda tool. Their use in *Animal Farm* reflects both the political nature of the novel and the simple style used in fables. They have an important function in reducing complex political ideologies into simple soundbites that are easily understood by the animals. They are encouraged by the pigs as they are seen to motivate individuals and to encourage the animals to work harder (e.g. Boxer's two mottos 'I will work harder' and 'Napoleon is always right').

Slogans are first used in old Major's speech, when he tells the animals that 'All animals are equal.' Snowball reduces the Seven Commandments to the single maxim of 'Four legs good, two legs bad' and slogans are seen again during the internal power struggle between Snowball and Napoleon over the building of the windmill.

Most noticeably, slogans are used to stifle discussion and opposition and to deflect criticism away from the pigs. They are also used to deceive the animals into thinking all is well ('All animals are equal'). Napoleon is glorified and his position as dictator is reinforced by the use of slogans ('Our Leader, Comrade Napoleon').

GRADE **BOOSTER**

Is Orwell using slogans and mottos to criticise politics in our society, where debate and ideology are reduced to such simplistic levels? (The *Communist Manifesto* sums up communism in four words: 'Abolition of private property'.) Considering alternative interpretations is important if you wish to achieve the higher grades.

Even the song 'Beasts of England' becomes discredited as the novel develops. Clover, who does not have the power of language to express her thoughts, continues to gain some comfort from singing the song that signifies the cause to her, until Squealer informs her in Chapter 7 that the song has been banned. It cannot be allowed to become any kind of rallying call for a return to how things were just after the Rebellion.

Orwell allows Clover's thoughts to be seen and in them he contrasts the dystopian reality with the utopian ideals of the Rebellion. The dystopian world is described clearly for us through Clover's unspoken thoughts, which, as we have seen, can be interpreted as an important indicator in understanding how the pigs gained control so easily.

The lower animals' inability to express their thoughts aloud, and therefore to question the information delivered by Squealer, demonstrates their linguistic weakness, which in turn limits their power. Orwell highlights the way education has been denied them, being provided mainly to the pigs.

By Chapter 10, Napoleon's hold over the animals is complete. Many of the commandments have been broken and the pigs and dogs enjoy a comfortable life while the other animals suffer. Orwell presents a dystopian world where the ideals of Chapters 1 and 2 have been corrupted but no one except Benjamin, who refuses to talk, can remember. Once Napoleon has gained power, Squealer works tirelessly to produce propaganda in order to cement and strengthen Napoleon's position as leader of the farm.

Closely linked to the use of propaganda is the establishment of a personality cult. A cult of personality developed around Stalin and he accepted many grandiloquent titles, for example, 'The Coryphaeus of Science', 'Father of Nations', 'Brilliant Genius of Humanity', 'Great Architect of Communism', 'Gardener of Human Happiness'. In addition, numerous villages, towns and cities were renamed after him. In a similar way Napoleon is given ever-more-ridiculous-sounding titles: 'Duckling's friend', 'Father of all animals', 'Protector of the sheep-fold' and 'Terror of Mankind.' He is also given credit for every successful achievement on the farm. The cows exclaim that the drinking water tastes excellent thanks to Napoleon and a hen boasts that under Napoleon's guidance she has laid six eggs in five days. His heroic status is further enhanced when he is given full credit for achieving victory at the Battle of the Cowshed.

The pigs give themselves more and more luxuries – moving into the farmhouse, drinking whisky and Napoleon eating from the Crown Derby dinner service – while the life of the other animals gets harder and harder. Napoleon becomes more and more remote and orders are issued through Squealer or one of the other pigs. Napoleon has separate apartments and eats alone. When he does appear in public, it is with great pomp and ceremony. He is always attended by his bodyguards, the dogs, and a black cockerel marches in front, acting as a trumpeter before he speaks.

Key quotation

'The birds did not understand Snowball's long words but they accepted his explanation…'

Key quotation

'The others said of Squealer that he could turn black into white.'

Build critical skills

Orwell wrote that the taking of the milk was supposed to be the 'turning point' of the novel. Why do you think he felt this?

Another method of propaganda is to blame the enemy for any problems or failings. Thus Snowball is said to be in league with either Mr Pilkington or Mr Frederick, depending on who is the current enemy at the time. When a violent storm destroys the half-built windmill, Snowball is blamed. Later, he is blamed for everything that goes wrong on the farm, from a broken window to a lost key.

Truth and lies

As part of a strategy that includes blaming the enemy (usually Snowball or the neighbouring farmers) and gaining credit for all achievements, dictators are normally very adept at rewriting history. (It is said that history is not what has actually happened, but is what is written by the victors.) Napoleon relies on the poor collective memories, trusting nature and gullibility of the other animals to achieve this. The most obvious example of this is the changing of the Seven Commandments. For example, when the pigs move into the farmhouse and start sleeping in beds, Boxer passes it off 'as usual with "Napoleon is always right!"' but 'Clover had not remembered that the Fourth Commandment mentioned sheets' but she quickly accepts that 'as it was there on the wall, it must have done so'. The barn wall serves as a symbol of collective memory that is gradually changed and eroded by the pigs.

> **GRADE** *BOOSTER*
>
> ```
> Note how Orwell chooses Boxer and Clover to voice their
> opinions on the changes in the Fourth Commandment. Why
> do you think he specifically chose these two animals?
> Think about who they represent. Being aware that
> Orwell is constantly consciously crafting the novel,
> that nothing happens by chance, is an important way to
> gain the higher grades.
> ```

Other changes to the commandments are either 'remembered wrong' or 'had slipped out of the animals' memory'. Snowball's part in the Battle of the Cowshed is not only diminished but the animals are told he was actually in league with Mr Jones at the time. His award of the 'Animal Hero, First Class' medal was simply a 'legend' spread by Snowball himself. The animals are told that the real hero of the battle and saviour of the farm was, of course, Napoleon.

The novel shows the way in which history is rewritten by the pigs, with very few animals surviving at the end to recall distant events. Orwell makes clear the way in which Squealer gets the animals to question and doubt their memories so that they end up forgetting the past. We see him turning 'black into white' as he manipulates the animals into believing the rewritten history: 'Do you not remember how, just at the moment when Jones and his men had got inside the yard, Snowball suddenly turned and fled, and many animals followed him?'

By doing this, Orwell shows the way in which the past and future are controlled by those who hold power in the present. As he said in his novel *Nineteen Eighty-Four*, 'Who controls the past controls the future; who controls the present controls the past.'

Totalitarianism

Any savage use of violence to control the populace will result in totalitarianism. This can be defined as a system of government that demands absolute control over all aspects of life and violently suppresses all opposing political ideologies. Total, unquestioning obedience to the leader is required.

> **Build critical skills**
>
> By commenting on the effect that specific words and phrases have on the reader, you are showing that you have an appreciation of the writer's skill. How does the phrase 'there was a pile of corpses lying before Napoleon's feet and the air was heavy with the smell of blood' create a sense of horror and disgust?

When Napoleon announces that the 'Sunday morning Meetings would come to an end' and all decisions would be taken by a 'special committee, presided over by himself', he is ending all pretence of collective decision making ('there would be no more debates') and thus strengthening his grip on the farm. Meetings, debates and voting, all ideas associated with democracy, are banned and are replaced with parades and speeches. The irony of Napoleon ordering 'Spontaneous Demonstrations' is lost on the animals. The intention of these processions and speeches is twofold: to fool the animals into believing that they 'were truly their own masters' and also to cause the animals, at least for a while, to forget their constant hunger.

As only Squealer communicates and explains the pigs' decisions, the animals are kept in ignorance of the truth: they only hear, and thus believe, what Napoleon wants them to hear. The various animal committees established by Snowball to educate the animals are no more and instead, under the guise of education, the animals are fed propaganda that supports Napoleon's ideas and justifies his actions. Thus, before the pigs emerge on two legs, Squealer takes control of the sheep and tells the other animals that he is 'teaching them a new song'. When the pigs emerge from the farmhouse, walking on their hind legs, the sheep help to silence any protest by their constant bleating of 'Four legs

Key quotation

'Sometimes the older ones among them racked their dim memories and tried to determine whether in the early days of the Rebellion, when Jones's expulsion was still recent, things had been better or worse than now. They could not remember.'

Key quotation

'They found it comforting that they were their own masters and that the work they did was for their own benefit.'

Key quotation

'they were able to forget that their bellies were empty, at least part of the time.'

Key quotation

'Napoleon ... said that ... the education of the young was more important.'

good, two legs *better*!' In the early days of the Rebellion, Napoleon uses the cover of education to hide the real reason for his seclusion of the nine puppies, the same puppies who become savage killers, representing the Secret Police of Stalin's Russia.

The exploitation of the workers is a key feature of totalitarianism and throughout *Animal Farm* we constantly see the animals being exploited by the pigs. It perhaps starts with Napoleon drinking the milk while the other animals gather in the harvest and is best summed up by Mr Pilkington's speech at the end of the novel, praising Napoleon's achievements in exploiting the animals for the pigs' benefit.

Key quotation

'the lower animals on Animal Farm did more work and received less food than any animals in the county.'

> **GRADE** *BOOSTER*
>
> Showing an appreciation of the writer's skill, for example by commenting on the effect of a specific word, is essential to achieve the higher grades. What does the word 'lower' imply about Mr Pilkington's and Napoleon's attitude to the other animals in the following comment: 'If you have your lower animals to contend with ... we have our lower classes'?

The ironically phrased 'strictly voluntary' work on Sunday afternoons is another clear example of exploitation – if any animal didn't work on the Sunday afternoon, his rations were reduced by half. The way Boxer is treated is the most cynical example of exploitation. He literally works himself almost to death, believing it is for the good of every animal on the farm. Once he has lost his usefulness, the pigs sell him to the knackers and buy a crate of whisky with the proceeds of the sale.

In his essay 'Literature and Totalitarianism', Orwell wrote that totalitarianism 'abolished freedom of thought' by telling people what to think. The reduction of the Seven Commandments to one maxim is an example of the way in which the animals' thoughts are limited by the pigs. When Napoleon gets the sheep on his side and they bleat continuously in meetings, we see the way in which their blindness also erodes freedom of speech. In the last chapter, this is made apparent when Orwell writes that the animals, despite their lack of power over language, 'might have uttered some word of protest.

Key quotation

'Instead they had come to a time when no one dared speak his mind ... when you had to watch your comrades torn to pieces after confessing to shocking crimes.'

But just at that moment, as though at a signal, all the sheep burst out into a tremendous bleating of – "Four legs good, two legs *better*!"...'

A totalitarian regime will allow no opposition and so the four young pigs, who had protested when Napoleon had abolished the Meetings, are killed by the dogs, as are the three hens who were the ringleaders in the unsuccessful rebellion over the eggs. When Animal Farm is proclaimed a Republic, the only candidate for leadership is Napoleon and he is elected unanimously.

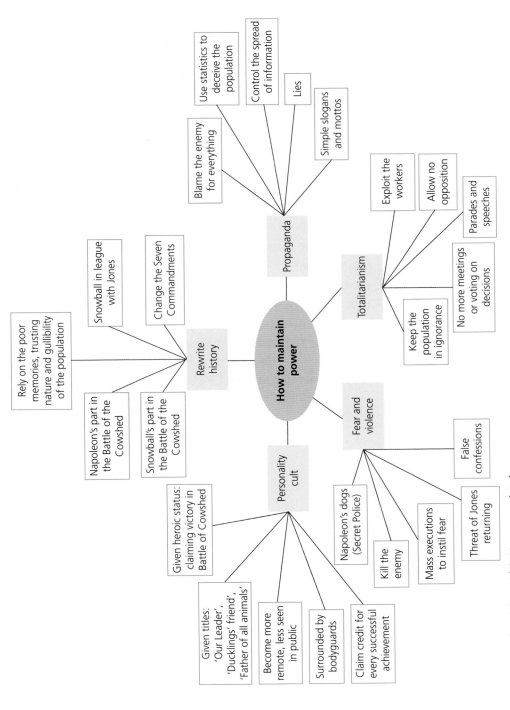

▲ Visual revision aid 2: How to maintain power

GRADE *FOCUS*

Grade 5

To achieve a Grade 5, students will reveal a clear understanding of the key themes of the novel and how Orwell uses language, form and structure to explore them, supported by appropriate references to the text.

Grade 8

To achieve a Grade 8, students will examine and evaluate the key themes of the novel, analysing the ways that Orwell uses language, form and structure to explore them. Comments will be supported by carefully chosen and well-integrated references to the text.

REVIEW YOUR LEARNING

(Answers are given on p. 103.)

1   What do we mean when we talk about the themes of a novel?

2   What are the themes in *Animal Farm* connected with?

3   Name five main themes that recur in *Animal Farm*.

4   Give two examples of ways in which Orwell suggests that control can be maintained over a society once power has been seized.

5   List events to show how the level of violence increases as the story unfolds.

6   Give an example of what Orwell wrote in *Nineteen Eighty-Four* concerning the rewriting of history that is also relevant to *Animal Farm*.

Language, style and analysis

Target your thinking

- Why is Orwell's use of language important? (**AO2**)
- How important is the setting in *Animal Farm*? (**AO1, AO2**)
- How does the author use language, style and structure to convey his message? (**AO2, AO3**)

Language

All authors choose their words carefully and purposefully for maximum effect, even when the language appears simple, as is the case with *Animal Farm*. This appearance can be deceptive as Orwell uses many language devices to tell the story. The straightforward prose style is appropriate for a fable or fairy story (see below) and Orwell deliberately uses some of the methods we associate with those forms of story.

> **GRADE BOOSTER**
>
> In an exam answer you may wish to consider the possibility that if Orwell is criticising people's unquestioning beliefs in political ideologies that can be reduced to simple slogans, then can't the same criticism be levelled at *Animal Farm*? Exploring alternative interpretations like this is a great way to gain the higher levels.

With his use of an external narrator, Orwell provides us with a traditional storyteller who unfolds the story for us. He opens the story with a focus on character and setting, before moving on to events which, as we have seen, relate to history. The narrator signals time passing and events for us in a simplified way: 'Three nights later old Major died peacefully in his sleep'; 'All through that summer'; 'By the late summer'.

Apart from Chapter 10, which takes place after 'Years [have] passed', the events in the novel span four years:

- Summer, Year 1: Chapters 1–4
- Autumn, Year 1: Chapter 4
- Winter, Year 1: Chapter 5
- Spring, Year 2: Chapter 5
- Winter, Year 2: Chapter 6
- Spring, Year 3: Chapter 7
- Autumn, Year 3: Chapter 8
- Winter, Year 3: Chapter 8
- Summer, Year 4: Chapter 8

Repetition

One method Orwell employs is repetition, which is a very common device in fairy stories – think of 'The Three Little Pigs' or 'Goldilocks and the Three Bears'. In *Animal Farm* the use of repetition has precise purposes. The frequent mention of the animals' bad memories reminds us of how easy it is for the pigs to rewrite history. The constant bleating of the sheep has three functions: at text level it drowns out all attempts at criticism, but it is also used by Orwell to satirise people's unquestioning beliefs in political ideologies. Finally, it can be seen as a criticism of political systems that reduce complex ideas to simple slogans.

Boxer's maxims of 'I will work harder' and 'Napoleon is always right' are another example of Orwell's use of repetition. These help to emphasise the blind faith people have in their rulers: any failings in the system can be solved by working harder (meaning the working classes, not the rulers, of course!) and we must never criticise our 'betters'! Boxer's stupidity is also highlighted by the use of these maxims: this can most clearly be seen when, after the mass executions, Boxer's only response is 'I do not understand … it must be due to some fault in ourselves. The solution … is to work harder.' Squealer cynically uses Boxer's motto when he tells the animals that Boxer's 'very last words' were 'Napoleon is always right'. Napoleon too uses these maxims for his own ends in his oration in Boxer's honour, telling every animal that each 'would do well to adopt [these maxims] as his own'.

Another example of Orwell deliberately using repetition is the ironic use of the word 'comrades'. Here he is mocking the Communist regime's use of the word – the pigs and animals clearly are not comrades.

Orwell uses a list to convey the horror of the dystopian world that the animals endure post rebellion: lack of free speech, terror and murder. He uses emotive language to emphasise the sadness of the situation, with words such as 'fierce', 'growling' and 'shocking' conveying the absolute fear faced by the animals. The lack of freedom in this dystopian world is emphasised through the words 'had to', and the inclusion of the word 'comrades' is an ironic reminder of the utopian ideals of the Rebellion.

Build critical skills

Sometimes the word order, as well as the words themselves, is significant. Why do you think Orwell places the words 'silent' and 'terrified' at the beginning rather than at the end of this sentence?

After Snowball has been chased off the farm: 'Silent and terrified, the animals crept back into the barn.'

What is the effect of having these two words at the beginning? Find one more example of Orwell using word order for particular emphasis.

The narrative voice

An important aspect of language used in a story is the narrative voice used by the author. The narrative voice is the method the writer uses to tell the story. Most stories are told in the third person, that is, by an ever-present narrator who knows everything about the characters and events. *Animal Farm* is written in this way but with a slight, but interesting, difference. Orwell, at times, chooses not to tell us everything but instead leaves his readers to infer for themselves what has happened. Often significant events are not narrated by this omniscient voice but instead are seen through the eyes of the animals. For example: '…the animals were satisfied that they had been mistaken' when Squealer is caught altering the Fifth Commandment; it is described as a 'strange incident which hardly anyone was able to understand'. The effect of describing events through the eyes of the animals is that it emphasises their ignorance and gullibility and prompts the reader to ask why, if it is so obvious to us, they can't see what is happening?

Through this narrative viewpoint, Orwell invites the reader to deduce the significance of events and comments ironically. For example, after Squealer's propagandist explanation regarding the milk and apples, Orwell comments that 'The importance of keeping the pigs in good health was all too obvious.' As well as mocking the stupidity of the animals here, Orwell leads the reader to despair of any hope that the ideals of Animalism can succeed.

> **Build critical skills**
>
> Why do you think that Orwell does not tell us what has happened to the disappearing milk but simply states that when the animals came back from the harvest 'it was noticed that the milk had disappeared'?

> **GRADE BOOSTER**
>
> It is no good just knowing the type of narrative voice employed; it is essential to explain in your responses **why** Orwell uses this method, what effect it has on the way the story is told and how it helps Orwell convey his message to the reader.

Squealer's voice uses a combination of strategies that both simplify and complicate language. By radically simplifying language and indoctrinating the sheep when he teaches them to bleat 'Four legs good, two legs *better*!' he limits the terms of debate and ensures the pigs' control. Similarly, by complicating language unnecessarily and using statistics and clever wording (such as his reference to 'tactics' in Chapter 5), he confuses and intimidates the uneducated animals. When he explains that the rations have been 'readjusted' rather than 'reduced', and when he tells the animals all that Napoleon does is for the good of the farm, he is manipulating them into accepting what he says as truth. Squealer's ability to manipulate language is apparent from the start and we see in his speeches the ways he uses persuasive devices to good effect. His rhetorical questions, lists, choices of inclusion and omission and personal pronouns are all tools that help to pacify the animals and maintain the pigs' power.

The animals all have their own distinctive voices. For example, Orwell often has Squealer pose a number of rhetorical questions, causing the animals to question their own memories and suspicions of the pigs. He uses personal pronouns such as 'you' repeatedly in an accusatory way, inferring that the animals are in the wrong to want the pigs not to have a proper rest or sleep in beds. Orwell has Squealer refer to the animals as 'comrades' and uses the personal pronoun 'we' to suggest that he is on their side. His reference to the animals' absolute need for the pigs and their 'brainwork', along with Orwell's use of the emotive word 'surely', provokes guilt and instils a fear in the animals that without the pigs, Jones would come back to rule the farm. By mentioning Jones, Squealer ensures that the animals' fear of a past master keeps their present one in control.

It is noticeable that while Orwell frequently uses direct speech when the animals are talking, Napoleon's speech is always written in reported speech and never given in direct speech. This has the effect of making Napoleon seem a more remote figure, distant and aloof from the rest of the animals. The personality cult that has been built up around him is also emphasised when he never gives direct orders himself but always uses one of the pigs, usually Squealer, to convey his orders: he is seen by the animals as being too important actually to talk to them.

Realistic detail

Orwell writes very concisely, often using multiple adjectives to give the reader a lot of information very quickly. For example, Mollie is a 'foolish, pretty, white mare' and Clover a 'stout, motherly mare'. He often adds precise realistic detail, for example the effect of the seasons on the farm, which Orwell often uses to highlight the difficulties the farm faces: 'the autumn producing thirty-one young pigs' (which would have to be fed), or the description of Boxer and Clover setting down their 'vast hairy hoofs with great care lest there should be some small animal concealed in the straw'. The effect of such detail is, ironically, to add realism to what is a fable not a realistic story, helping us to suspend our disbelief and so be more receptive to the story and its message.

Imagery and symbolism

The vocabulary and sentence structure of *Animal Farm* is very simple, as is fitting for a novel that Orwell subtitled *A Fairy Story*. The simplicity of the story's style does not lend itself to an abundance of imagery, meaning that when Orwell does introduce imagery it is all the more effective.

A good example of this is the beginning of Chapter 6: 'All that year the animals worked like slaves.' This is a common image but in the context of this novel it is a powerful ironic comment: actually the animals are not *like* slaves — they *are* slaves, although they do not know it.

> **GRADE BOOSTER**
>
> If you are asked about symbolism in the text, you could discuss Animal Farm's flag, with its image of hoof and horn. Mentioning that this is similar to the Red Banner's image of the hammer and sickle (used by the Bolsheviks as a symbol of their ideological commitment to placing all authority in the hands of workers and peasants) may gain you extra marks in an exam.

Of course the entire novel is rich in symbolism, but it can be useful sometimes to consider some of the symbols that are also potent images, for example the flag. Flags are symbols of patriotism or loyalty to a geographical area, an organisation or a particular ideal. The hoof-and-horn flag is particularly interesting. Its background is green, perhaps suggesting the peace and tranquillity of pasture. It is therefore ironic that after the Rebellion the animals work just as hard and are treated as badly as in Jones's day. The flag later comes to represent the absolute control of the pigs when the hoof and horn are removed and it becomes a plain green flag.

Similarly, the whip is used to symbolise the cruel oppression of the animals by Jones. The destruction of the whips at the birth of Animal Farm is a triumphant moment for the animals — 'All the animals capered with joy when they saw the whips going up in flames' — but Clover is terrified towards the end of the novel when she sees Napoleon walking on his hind legs with a whip in his trotter.

> **GRADE BOOSTER**
>
> There is little point in being able simply to identify or list various aspects of language, style and structure. You need to be able to comment on how they add to the novel and help Orwell get his message across to the reader.

Finally, the apples and milk can be seen as symbolic of the luxuries that the animals believed they would all share after the Rebellion. The fact that they are taken away is the first indication of the pigs' greed and their belief that they see themselves as superior to the other animals.

Style

If the characters in a novel tell us *who*, the plot tells us *what* and the themes tell us *why*, then the style of a novel tells us *how* all these elements knit together to produce the text. The style of *Animal Farm* is particularly important in conveying Orwell's message. The story may be told in a straightforward way – but don't be fooled by its apparent simplicity. *Animal Farm* has a clearly defined style that is crucial to the author's purpose.

The most obvious aspect of the style is that the novel is written as a story with talking animals, like many children's stories. Orwell originally subtitled his novel *A Fairy Story* and there are clear aspects of fairy tales in *Animal Farm*: the simple plot and setting, the struggle between good and evil and the stereotypical characters.

In this novel, however, good does not triumph over evil and the novel does not end with our heroes and heroines living 'happily ever after'. Instead of utopia being achieved, we have a dystopian world being created. The advantages of using animals is that the storyline, and characters, are kept simple, allowing Orwell's message about corruption and abuse of power to be all the more clearly seen. This simple, easily understood nature of the story makes for wide audience appeal and easy translation into other languages.

Contrasting styles

At the text level, what appears to be a simplicity of the language can, on closer inspection, become ambiguous and the effect of this simplicity is sometimes deliberately reversed. Orwell, mostly through Squealer, resorts to jargon and 'scientific' explanations to convince, confuse and manipulate the animals. There are numerous examples in the text of the way in which language is used to maintain power. Most of the animals (with the exception of Benjamin) are unable to understand concepts and ideologies, and Squealer is able to exploit their inability to think in the abstract.

Snowball also resorts to similar methods. As early as Chapter 3, we see Snowball's superior linguistic ability when he uses words such as 'propulsion' and 'manipulation', which the birds do not understand, to convince the animals that a wing is a leg. Later we see Squealer using language as a device to maintain the pigs' power, when he talks of 'tactics' in Chapter 5, which the animals do not understand, and when we are told that he refers to 'mysterious things' called 'files', 'reports' and 'memoranda', with the implied suggestion that these are unintelligible to the animals.

Key quotation

'Milk and apples (this has been proved by Science, comrades) contain substances absolutely necessary to the well-being of a pig.'

Fable and allegory

The use of animals indicates that *Animal Farm* can be described as a fable and/or allegory. A fable is usually a story with animals that have the power of speech and have human characteristics. There is always a moral or message about the human condition in the story. *Aesop's Fables* are perhaps the most well-known, for example 'The Tortoise and the Hare', which shows that patience and perseverance are rewarded. An allegory is a text that has a meaning unrelated to the actual story. In effect, an allegory is like a metaphor except the representation is sustained throughout. Both allegories and fables have a very similar purpose and with regard to *Animal Farm* the two terms can be regarded as interchangeable.

The fable/allegorical elements in *Animal Farm* operate on two levels. The novel is an allegory of the events leading up to the Russian Revolution (1917) and the Communist regime that followed, up to the Tehran Conference in 1943. Characters and events in the novel relate closely to actual historical figures and events in Russian history. On a deeper level, however, the novel operates as a warning against tyranny, oppression and totalitarian regimes. Orwell is telling the reader that we must always be vigilant and hold our rulers to account.

Setting

The novel is set entirely on the farm, although there are passing references to other places: after the Rebellion Jones is to be found in The Red Lion pub, 'complaining to anyone who would listen'. Orwell also gives us brief descriptions of the two neighbouring farms and the pigeons bring news of Mollie being 'between the shafts of a smart dogcart' on the other side of Willington and of 'a wave of rebelliousness [that] ran through the countryside'. The simple reason for this concentration of events in one location is that *Animal Farm* is a satire on the Russian Revolution and the subsequent events in that country.

Within the farm itself there are various locations that have a particular significance:

1 The farmhouse is a symbol of fear for the animals, as it represents Jones and other humans. It is to be preserved as a museum, a reminder of the bad times when Jones was the master. Thus, when the pigs move into the farmhouse, Orwell is showing their corruption and abuse of power: by breaking this resolution, as well as the Fourth Commandment, they are becoming more and more like Jones.

2 The knoll, where the windmill was built, is the place the animals seem to congregate in moments of great joy (after the success of the Rebellion) or great sadness (after the mass executions). It is used

Key quotation

'This, said Squealer, was something called tactics. … "Tactics, comrades, tactics!" … The animals were not certain what the word meant, but … they accepted his explanation without further questions.'

Key quotation

'That was theirs too, but they were frightened to go inside.'

Build critical skills

How does Orwell show the animals' feelings when they enter the farmhouse for the first time?

Key quotation

'All were agreed that no animal must ever live there.'

Key quotation

'...they hurled
themselves into the
air in great leaps of
excitement.'

**Build critical
skills**

Compare how
Orwell shows the
contrast in the
animals' feelings
when they go to
the knoll after the
Rebellion with when
they go to the knoll
after the executions.

**Build critical
skills**

At the point just
after Snowball has
been driven out,
how does Orwell
emphasise the
difference between
the idealism of old
Major's speech and
the reality of life on
the farm?

Foreshadowing: a
technique used to warn
the reader of a future
event.

Key quotation

'They are taking Boxer
to the knacker's'

by Orwell to show how far life on the farm has moved away from
those early idealistic days when the animals were in 'ecstasy' with the
thought that everything 'they could see was theirs'.

3 The barn has great significance as it is the place where the first
meeting of the animals takes place and where the animals have their
'Meetings' each Sunday, until these are banned by Napoleon. It is also
the place where the mass executions take place, thus enabling Orwell
to contrast the hope generated by old Major's speech with the despair
felt after the 'trials' and executions ordered by Napoleon. The barn is
where the Seven Commandments are written, and of course rewritten
by Squealer, symbolising the rewriting of history by the pigs and the
collective memory loss of the other animals.

Language and structure

Orwell's use of language helps to convey a circular structure to the novel
by introducing parallels in his narrative.

Read this extract from old Major's speech at the beginning of the novel:

'...our lives are miserable, laborious, and short. We are born, we are
given just so much food as will keep the breath in our bodies, and
those of us who are capable of it are forced to work to the last atom
of our strength'

Now read this extract from Chapter 10, when years have passed. Is the
life of the animals any different than it was in Chapter 1?

'...They were generally hungry, they slept on straw, they drank from
the pool, they laboured in the fields; in winter they were troubled by
the cold, and in summer by the flies.'

Orwell employs the technique of **foreshadowing** to create a circular
structure. He offers the reader hints as to what will happen later in the
story. For example, read this extract from old Major's speech at the
beginning of the novel:

'You, Boxer, the very day that those great muscles of yours lose their
power, Jones will sell you to the knacker, who will cut your throat
and boil you down for the foxhounds.'

Now read this extract from Chapter 9, when Boxer has finally collapsed
through overwork and is taken away in a van, supposedly to hospital:

'Benjamin pushed her aside, and in the midst of a deadly silence
he read: "Alfred Simmonds, Horse Slaughterer and Glue Boiler,
Willington. Dealer in Hides and Bone-Meal. Kennels supplied".'

GRADE *FOCUS*

Grade 5

To achieve a Grade 5 students will show a clear understanding of the methods Orwell uses to create effects for the reader, supported by appropriate references to the text.

Grade 8

To achieve a Grade 8, students will be able to explore and analyse the methods Orwell uses to create effects for the reader, supported by carefully chosen and well-integrated references to the text.

REVIEW YOUR LEARNING

(Answers are given on pp. 103–104.)

1 What is the most obvious aspect of the style of *Animal Farm*?
2 What techniques does Orwell use to emphasise key themes?
3 What effect does the use of unusual word order in some sentences have?
4 What is *Animal Farm* an allegory of?
5 What is the effect of the circular structure of the novel?
6 What is 'foreshadowing'?
7 Identify an example of foreshadowing in the novel.
8 How many years do the first nine chapters cover?

Tackling the exams

Target your thinking

- What sorts of questions will you have to answer?
- What is the best way for you to plan your answer?
- How can you improve your grade?
- What do you have to do to achieve the highest grade?

Your response to a question on *Animal Farm* will be assessed in a 'closed-book' English literature examination. This means that you are not allowed to take copies of the examination text into the examination room. Different examination boards will test you in different ways and it is vital that you know on which paper the modern prose novel will be, so that you can be well prepared on the day of the examination.

Whichever board you are studying, the table on the next page explains in which paper and section the novel appears. It gives you information about the sort of question you will face and how you will be assessed.

Marking

The marking of your response will vary depending on the board your school or you have chosen. Each exam board has a slightly different mark scheme, consisting of a ladder of levels. The marks you achieve in each part of the examination will be converted to your final overall grade. Grades are numbered from 1 to 9, with 9 being the highest.

It is important that you familiarise yourself with the relevant mark scheme(s) for your examination. After all, how can you do well unless you know exactly what is required?

Assessment Objectives for individual assessments are explained in the next section of the guide (p. 81).

Approaching the examination question

First impressions

First, read the whole question and make sure you understand *exactly* what the task requires you to do. It is very easy in the highly pressured atmosphere of the examination room to misread a question – and this can be disastrous. Under no circumstances should you try to twist the question to match the one that you have spent hours revising or the one that you did brilliantly on in your mock exam!

Exam board	AQA	Edexcel	OCR
Paper and section	Paper 2 Section A	Paper 1 Section B	Paper 1 Section A
Type of question	One discursive essay-type question.	One essay-type question.	One extended response-style question split into two parts: • Part a): comparison of an extract from *Animal Farm* with a same-genre unseen extract. • Part b): a related question on *Animal Farm*.
Closed book?	Yes	Yes	Yes
Choice of question?	Yes. Choose one question from a choice of two.	Yes. Choose one question from a choice of two.	No
Paper and section length	Paper 2: 2 hours 15 minutes. Section A: 40–45 minutes.	Paper 1: 1 hour 45 minutes. Section B: 50 minutes.	Paper 1: 2 hours. Section A: 1 hour 15 minutes Part a): 45 minutes Part b): 30 minutes
AOs assessed	AO1 AO2 AO3 AO4	AO1 AO3 AO4	AO1 AO2 AO3
Is AO4 (SPaG) assessed in this section?	Yes	Yes	No
Percentage of whole grade	20%	25%	25%

How to read the question

Are you being asked to think about how a character or a theme is being presented? Make sure you know so that you will be able to sustain your focus later.

Look carefully at any bullet points you are given. They are there to help and guide you.

Three exam boards offer *Animal Farm* as a text. Two (AQA and Edexcel) use an essay-type question. The wordings and formats of the questions are slightly different, however. OCR uses an extract-based question and comparison with an unseen text.

As a starting point, you may wish to underline keywords in the question, such as 'how' to remind you to write about methods, and any other words that you feel will help you focus on answering the question you are being asked.

Below you can see examples of the question type from each examination board, annotated in this way.

AQA

How does Orwell present humour in the novel to get his message across to the reader?

Write about:

- how the incidents you choose are humorous
- Orwell's message and his purpose in using humour in the novel. [30 marks]

[SPaG 4 marks]

Edexcel

Your response will be marked for a range of appropriate vocabulary and sentence structures, and accurate use of spelling and punctuation.

'Napoleon acted swiftly and ruthlessly. He ordered the hens' rations to be stopped, and decreed that any animal giving so much as a grain of corn to a hen should be punished by death.'

Explore how Napoleon is a leader to be feared but not respected.

You **must** refer to the context of the novel in your answer.

[40 marks (includes 8 marks for a range of appropriate vocabulary and sentence structures, and for accurate use of spelling and punctuation)]

OCR

For Part a), you should focus only on the extracts here rather than referring to the rest of your studied text.

a Compare how the effects of propaganda are presented in these two extracts. You should consider:

- the situations faced by the characters
- how the characters react to their situations
- how the writers' use of language and techniques creates effects.

[20 marks]

AND

b Explore another moment in *Animal Farm* that shows how Squealer uses propaganda to control the other animals. [20 marks]

Spot the differences!

- AQA and Edexcel both give a choice of questions to answer.
- Only AQA focuses on 'how' in its question. Edexcel gives a short extract as a stimulus and uses the term 'explore', while AQA directs you to 'write about' and gives two bullet points to guide your responses.
- Edexcel refers directly to the need to refer to the 'context' of the novel.
- Only Edexcel does not assess AO2 in this section.
- The questions from AQA are marked out of 34 (up to 30 marks for your answer and up to 4 marks for SPaG). The questions from Edexcel are marked out of 40 (up to 32 marks for your answer and up to 8 marks for SPaG). For OCR there are 40 marks available in Section A: 20 marks each for Parts a) and b).

'Working' the text for OCR

Read both passages carefully, underlining or highlighting any words or short phrases that you think might be related to the focus of the question and are of special interest. For example, they might be surprising, unusual or amusing. You might have a strong emotional or analytical reaction to them or you might think that they are particularly clever or noteworthy.

These words/phrases may work together to produce a particular effect, or to get you to think about a particular theme, or to explore the methods the writer uses to present a character in a particular way for their own purposes. You may pick out examples of literary techniques such as lists or use of imagery, or sound effects such as alliteration or onomatopoeia. You may spot an unusual word order, sentence construction or use of punctuation. The important thing to remember is that when you start writing you must try to *explain the effects* created by these words/phrases or techniques, and not simply identify what they mean. Remember that you are being asked to compare ideas and how they are presented in the two extracts. Above all, ensure that you are answering the question that has been asked.

Planning your answer

It is advisable to write a brief plan before you start writing your response to avoid repeating yourself or getting into a muddle. A plan is not a first draft. You will not have time to do this. In fact, if your plan consists of any full sentences at all, you are probably eating into the time you have available for writing a really insightful and considered answer.

A plan is important, however, because it helps you to gather and organise your thoughts, but it should consist only of brief words and phrases.

You may find it helpful to use a diagram of some sort – perhaps a spider diagram or flow chart. This may help you keep your mind open to new ideas as you plan, so that you can slot them in. Arranging your thoughts is then a simple matter of numbering the branches in the best possible order. Or you could make a list instead. The important thing is to choose a method that works for *you*.

The other advantage of having a plan is that if you run out of time, the examiner can look at the plan and may be able to give you an extra mark or two based on what you were about to do next.

Writing your answer

Now you are ready to start writing your answer. The first thing to remember is that you are working against the clock and so it's really important to use your time wisely.

It is possible that you may not have time to deal with all the points you wish to make in your response. If you simply identify several language features and make a brief comment on each, you will be working at a fairly low level. The idea is to select the ones that you find most interesting and develop them in a sustained and detailed manner. In order to move up the levels in the mark scheme, it is important to write a lot about a little, rather than a little about a lot.

You must also remember to address the whole question as you will be penalised if you fail to do so.

Part of exam technique is making sure that the examiner knows that you are developing an argument. You can make this clear by using 'signal words' to signpost your argument.

GRADE *BOOSTER*

Avoid beginning your essay by spelling out exactly what you intend to do ('In this essay I will show that…'): just get on with it.

GRADE *BOOSTER*

Your entire essay builds an argument based on evidence, like a lawyer in court arguing a case, so writing and structuring your essay well and providing evidence is very important.

If you have any time left at the end of the examination, do not waste it! Check carefully that your meaning is clear and that you have done the very best you can. Look back at your plan and check that you have included all your best points. Is there anything else you can add? Keep thinking until you are told to put your pen down!

Referring to the author and title

You can refer to Orwell either by name (make sure you spell it correctly) or as 'the writer' or 'the author'. You should never use his first name (George) – this sounds as if you know him personally. You can also save time by giving the novel title in full the first time you refer to it, and afterwards simply referring to it as 'the novel'.

Important!

If you are answering a question for AQA or OCR, do not lose sight of the author in your essay. Remember that the novel is a construct – the characters, their thoughts, their words, their actions have all been created by Orwell – so most of your points need to be about what Orwell might have been trying to achieve. In explaining how his message is conveyed to you, for instance through an event, something about a character, use of symbolism, personification, irony and so on, don't forget to mention his name. For example:

- Orwell makes it clear that…
- It is evident from … that Orwell is inviting the reader to consider…
- Here, the reader may well feel that Orwell is suggesting…

Writing in an appropriate style

Remember that you are expected to write in a suitable **register**. This means that you need to use an appropriate style. This means:

- *not* using colloquial language or slang, e.g. 'Squealer is a nasty piece of work. A bit of a toe-rag really.' (The only exception is when quoting directly from the text.)
- *not* becoming too personal, e.g. 'Boxer is like my mate, right, 'cos he…'
- using suitable phrases for an academic essay, e.g. 'It could be argued that…', *not* 'I reckon that…'
- *not* being too dogmatic – don't say 'This means that…'; it is much better to say 'This might suggest that…'

You are also expected to be able to use a range of technical terms correctly. If you can't remember the correct name for a technique, however, but can still describe its effect, you should still go ahead and do so.

> **GRADE** *BOOSTER*
>
> If you can't decide whether a phrase is a **simile** or a **metaphor**, it helps to just refer to it as an example of imagery and explain how the author wants the reader to respond to the word-picture he is painting.

Simile: a comparison using the words 'as' or 'like'.
Metaphor: a comparison that doesn't use 'as' or 'like' but instead says something is something else.

The first person ('I')

It is perfectly appropriate to say 'I feel' or 'I think'. You are being asked for *your* opinion. Just remember that you are being asked for your opinion about *what* Orwell may have been trying to convey in his novel (his themes and ideas) and *how* he does this (through the characters, events, language, form and structure of the novel).

Spelling, punctuation and grammar (AO4)

Your spelling, punctuation and grammar (SPaG) are specifically targeted for assessment on modern prose by AQA and Edexcel, so you cannot afford to forget that you will demonstrate your grasp of the novel through the way you write. Take great care with this and don't be careless. If the examiner cannot understand what you are trying to say, they will not be able to give you credit for your ideas.

GRADE *BOOSTER*

It is important to make the individual quotations you select brief and to try to *embed* them. This will save you time, enabling you to develop your points at greater depth and so raise your grade. To check how good you are at embedding quotations, read your sentences out to someone who has not read the novel. See if they can tell where Orwell's words begin and end. If they cannot, you have integrated his words smoothly.

How to raise your grade

The most important advice is to answer the question that is in front of you, and to start doing so promptly. When writing essays in other subjects, you may have been taught to write a lengthy, elegant introduction explaining what you are about to do. In the literature examination, though, you have only a short time so it is best to get started as soon as you have gathered your thoughts together and made a brief plan.

Sometimes students panic because they don't know how to start. It is absolutely fine to begin your response with words from the question itself; in fact this will help you to focus your response on the question.

What methods has the writer used? Although there is a whole range of methods with which you need to be familiar, it might be something as simple as a powerful adjective. What do you think is the impact of that word? It might be that the word you are referring to has more than one meaning. If that's the case, the examiner will be impressed if you can discuss what the word means to you, but are also able to suggest other meanings. Is context relevant here? In other words, what might Orwell be saying about dictators? What might Orwell have been trying to express about fear or respect when he chose a particular word or phrase? Is there an actual overall effect? For instance, Orwell often uses **irony** to suggest how the animals are deceived and controlled by the pigs.

Be very careful about lapsing into narrative. If you are asked about how Orwell presents Napoleon, remember that the focus of the question is about the methods that Orwell uses. Do not simply tell the examiner what Napoleon does or what he is like – this is a very common mistake.

Irony: when the reader knows something that characters (in this case, the animals) are not aware of, thus involving the reader more closely in the novel.

GRADE *BOOSTER*

It is really important that you show an awareness of the novel as a constructed work. Make clear that you know that this is a novel and that the characters are constructs through which Orwell expresses his thoughts and ideas. To do this, you need to foreground the writer, using statements such as:

- Orwell highlights…
- The author makes clear…
- He elaborates…
- The author portrays…
- He illustrates…
- Orwell reinforces…
- He shows…
- He demonstrates…

GRADE *FOCUS*

Grade 5

- Candidates have a clear focus on the text and the task and are able to 'read between the lines'.
- Candidates develop a clear understanding of the ways in which writers use language, form and structure to create effects for the readers.
- Candidates use a range of detailed textual evidence to support comments.
- Candidates use understanding of the idea that both writers and readers may be influenced by where, when and why a text is produced.
- Candidates make relevant comparisons between the ways writers use language, structure and form, as well as some comparison of effects on readers (OCR Part a).

Grade 8

- Candidates produce a consistently convincing, informed response to a range of meanings and ideas within the text.
- Candidates use ideas that are well linked and often build on one another.

- Candidates dig deep into the text, examining, exploring and evaluating the writer's use of language, form and structure.
- Candidates carefully select finely judged textual references that are well integrated in order to support and develop responses to texts.
- Candidates show perceptive understanding of how contexts shape texts and responses to texts.
- Candidates explore comparisons of the ways that writers make use of language, structure and form, as well as insightful comparisons of the effects on readers (OCR Part b).

Achieving a Grade 9

To reach the very highest level you need to have thought about the novel more deeply and produced a response that is conceptualised, critical and exploratory at a deeper level. You might, for instance, challenge accepted critical views in evaluating whether the writer has always been successful. If, for example, you think Orwell set out to create sympathy for the working classes, how successful do you think he has been?

You may feel that the creation of sympathy for the working classes through what might be described as the blatant manipulation of the reader's emotional response to Boxer's death alienates some modern readers. Does the presentation of Boxer verge on sentimentality, and if so do you consider this a problem?

You need to make original points clearly and succinctly and to convince the examiner that your viewpoint is really your own, and a valid one, with constant and careful reference to the text. This will be aided by the use of short and apposite (really relevant) quotations, skilfully embedded in your answer along the way (see 'Sample essays' section, p. 86).

REVIEW YOUR LEARNING

(Answers are given on p. 104.)

1 Will you be assessed on spelling, punctuation and grammar in your response to *Animal Farm*?

2 Can you take your copy of the novel into the exam?

3 Why is it important to plan your answer?

4 What should you do if you finish ahead of time?

5 Give an example of a keyword to look for in the question.

6 Give two examples of 'signal' words that signpost your argument or link paragraphs together.

All GCSE examinations are pinned to specific areas of learning that the examiners want to be sure candidates have mastered. These are known as Assessment Objectives or AOs. If you are studying *Animal Farm* as an examination text for AQA, OCR or Edexcel, the examiner marking your exam response will be trying to give you marks, using the particular mark scheme for that board. All mark schemes, however, are based on fulfilling the key AOs for English literature.

Assessment Objectives

The Assessment Objectives that apply to your response to *Animal Farm* are shown below.

For AQA, OCR and Edexcel:

> **AO1** Read, understand and respond to texts. Students should be able to:
> - maintain a critical style and develop an informed personal response
> - use textual references, including quotations, to support and illustrate interpretations.

For AQA and OCR only:

> **AO2** Analyse the language, form and structure used by a writer to create meanings and effects, using relevant subject terminology where appropriate.

For AQA, OCR and Edexcel:

> **AO3** Show understanding of the relationship between texts and the contexts in which they were written.

For AQA and Edexcel only:

> **AO4** Use a range of vocabulary and sentence structures for clarity, purpose and effect, with accurate spelling and punctuation. (You can't forget about it entirely but if your spelling or punctuation leaves something to be desired at least you can lift your spirits by reminding yourself that AO4 is only worth about 5% of your total mark!)

What skills do you need to show?

Let's break the Assessment Objectives down to see what they really mean.

> **AO1** Read, understand and respond to texts. Students should be able to:
> - maintain a critical style and develop an informed personal response
> - use textual references, including quotations, to support and illustrate interpretations.

At its most basic level, this AO is about having a good grasp of what a text is about and being able to express an opinion about it within the context of the question. For example, if you were to say, 'The novel is about animals taking over and running a farm by themselves' you would be beginning to address AO1 because you would have made a **personal response**. An '**informed**' response refers to the basis on which you make that judgement. In other words, you need to show that you know the novel well enough to answer the question.

AO1 also requires you to '**use textual references, including quotations, to support and illustrate interpretations**'. This means giving short direct quotations from the text. For example, if you wanted to support the idea that by the end of the novel the pigs had become the same as humans, you could use a direct quote to say that the other animals looked 'from pig to man' but that it was 'impossible to say which was which'. Alternatively, you can simply refer to details in the text, in order to support your views. So you might say 'the other animals were unable to tell the difference between the pigs and the humans'.

Generally speaking, most candidates find AO1 relatively straightforward. Usually, it is tackled well – if you answer the question you are asked, this Assessment Objective will probably take care of itself.

> **AO2** Analyse the language, form and structure used by a writer to create meanings and effects, using relevant subject terminology where appropriate.

AO2, however, is a different matter. Most examiners would probably agree that covering AO2 is a weakness for many candidates, particularly those students who only ever talk about the characters as if they were real people.

In simple terms, AO2 refers to the writer's methods and is often signposted in questions by the word 'how', e.g. in the phrase 'How does the writer present…'.

Overall AO2 is equal in importance to AO1 so it is vital that you are fully aware of this objective. The word '**language**' refers to Orwell's use of words. Remember that writers choose words very carefully in order to achieve particular effects. They may spend quite a long time deciding between two or three words that are similar in meaning in order to create the precise effect they are looking for.

If you are addressing AO2 in your response to *Animal Farm*, you will typically find yourself using Orwell's name and exploring the choices he has made. For example, Orwell describes the animals in Chapter 6 as working 'like slaves'; commenting on the effect of the word 'slaves' will set you on the right path to explaining why this is an interesting word choice. (Of course, there is no right or wrong answer but you might say that Orwell is being ironic here as the animals think they are free but actually they are enslaved to Napoleon and the pigs.) It is this explanation that addresses AO2, while 'The animals worked very hard' is a simple AO1 comment.

Language also encompasses a wide range of writer's methods, such as the use of different types of imagery, words that create sound effects, litotes, irony and so on.

AO2 also refers to your use of '**subject terminology**'. This means that you should be able to use terms such as 'metaphor', 'alliteration' and 'hyperbole' with confidence and understanding. Don't despair if you can't remember the term – you will still gain marks for explaining the effects being created!

The terms '**form**' and '**structure**' refer to the kind of text you are studying and how it has been 'put together' by the writer. This might include the narrative technique being used (in *Animal Farm* Orwell uses the third-person intrusive narrator); the genre(s) the text is part of; the order of events and the effects created by this order; and the way key events are juxtaposed.

For example, after the mass executions the animals gather together at the little knoll overlooking the farm. Orwell's beautiful description 'Never had the farm … appeared to the animals so desirable a place' follows on from the scene of carnage with 'a pile of corpses' and the air filled with 'the smell of blood'. It thus offers a powerful contrast. Effects of structure can also be seen in the writer's use of sentence lengths and word order (syntax).

Remember – if you do not address AO2 at all, it will be very difficult to achieve much higher than Grade 1, since you will not be answering the question.

> **AO3** Show understanding of the relationship between texts and the contexts in which they were written.

This AO, although not perhaps considered as important as AO1 and AO2, is still worth between 15 and 20 per cent of your total mark in the examination as a whole, and so should not be underestimated.

To cover AO3 you must show that you understand the links between a text and when, why and for whom it was written. For example, some awareness of the Russian Revolution and what happened when Stalin was in control will help you to understand Orwell's intentions in writing *Animal Farm* in order to help people know the truth about life in Russia under Stalin. Equally, some knowledge of Orwell's background might give you useful insight into his concern about the treatment of the working classes at that time.

You might also consider literary context. *Animal Farm* was written as a fable or allegory, so readers would know that it contained a moral or message from the author, rather than just an entertaining story.

Remember, however, that context should not be 'bolted on' to your response for no good reason; you are writing about literature not history!

> **AO4** Use a range of vocabulary and sentence structures for clarity, purpose and effect, with accurate spelling and punctuation.

This AO is fairly self-explanatory. It is worth remembering that it is assessed in your response to *Animal Farm* and that a clear and well-written response should always be your aim. If your spelling is so bad or your grammar and lack of punctuation so confusing that the examiner cannot understand what you are trying to express, this will obviously adversely affect your mark!

Similarly, although there are no marks awarded for good handwriting, and none taken away for untidiness or crossings-out, it is obviously important for the examiner to be able to read what you have written. If you believe your handwriting is so illegible that it may cause difficulties for the examiner, you need to speak to your school's examination officer in plenty of time before the exam. They may be able to arrange for you to have a scribe or to sit your examination using a computer.

What you will not gain many marks for

You will **not** gain many marks if you do the following:

- **Retell the story.** You can be sure that the examiner marking your response knows the story inside out. You will, at times, have to refer to a certain point in the book, but that should be focused and brief. A key feature of the lowest grades is 'retelling the story'. Don't do it.

- **Quote long passages.** Remember, the point is that every reference and piece of quotation must serve a very specific point you are making. If you quote at length, the examiner will have to guess which bit of the quotation you mean to serve your point. Don't impose work on the examiner – be explicit about exactly which words you have found specific meaning in. Keep quotes short and smart.

- **Merely identify literary devices.** You will never gain marks simply for identifying literary devices, such as the use of a simile or rhyme. You can gain marks, however, by identifying these features, exploring the reasons you think the author has used them and offering a thoughtful consideration of how they might impact on the reader, as well as giving an evaluation of how effective you think they are.

- **Give unsubstantiated opinions.** The examiner will be keen to give you marks for your opinions, but only if they are supported by reasoned argument and references to the text.

- **Write about characters as if they are real people.** It is important to remember that characters are constructs – the writer is responsible for what the characters do and say. Don't ignore the author!

REVIEW YOUR LEARNING

(Answers are given on p. 104.)

1 What is AO1 assessing?
2 What is AO2 assessing?
3 What is AO3 assessing?
4 What is AO4 assessing?
5 Which exam board specification are you following and what AOs should you be focusing on?
6 What should you *not* do in your responses?

Sample essays

The question below is a typical AQA character-based question and is also similar to an Edexcel question in requiring an essay-type answer.

> How does Orwell use the character of Boxer to explore ideas about betrayal and the corrupting influence of power in *Animal Farm*?
>
> Write about:
> - how Orwell presents the character of Boxer in the novel
> - how Orwell uses the character of Boxer to present ideas about betrayal and the corrupting influence of power in the novel.

Student X, who is working at around Grade 5, begins their response like this (please note that sample Grade 5 responses may contain errors in spelling, punctuation and grammar):

1 This kind of introduction, simply repeating the question, will gain no marks and takes up some valuable exam time.

In this answer I am going to explain how Orwell presents the character of Boxer and uses him to present ideas about betrayal and corrupting influence of power. Boxer is a huge carthorse, 'an enormous beast' who is very strong but also very gentle as he is sad when he thinks he has killed the stable boy. He is the most likeable character in 'Animal Farm' because of his hard work and commitment to the farm, which symbolises Russia. Orwell presents Boxer as a friendly but stupid animal because he has a white stripe down his face and never learns the alphabet beyond the letter 'D'. He is the most devoted follower of Animalism and always attends the secret meetings held in the barn.

2 Using quotations and close reference to the text to support points will gain marks.

After the Rebellion Boxer is an inspiration to all the other animals. Whenever there were difficulties Boxer was there and 'always pulled them through'. He was more like three horses than one. He got up half-an-hour earlier and worked later than anyone else. This makes the reader feel very sympathetic and full of admiration for Boxer who is devoting his life to the cause of Animalism. Orwell builds up sympathy and admiration for Boxer so that his betrayal and death are all the more shocking and arouse our hatred of the pigs even more.

3 Some understanding of the effects of the writer's methods on the reader.

This response has some positive features so far and suggests that the candidate is working at around Grade 5 of the AQA mark scheme, demonstrating 'clear understanding'.

Although this is a promising start to an exam essay, an even better response appears below. Student Y is working at the top end of the mark scheme. Carefully compare the differences between the two responses.

Boxer is one of the most significant characters in 'Animal Farm', not only because of the contribution he makes to Animalism, but also because in Orwell's allegory he is representative of the working class, the very people that the Rebellion was intended to benefit the most. Thus his betrayal by the pigs clearly reveals the corrupting influence of power. Although he is 'an enormous beast', Orwell presents him as gentle and caring – as when he and Clover take care not to step on any of the smaller animals and also in his reaction to the believed death of the stable lad, 'I have no wish to take life', which contrasts sharply with Snowball's reaction ('War is war. The only good human being is a dead one.'). Despite his great strength – he is as strong as two horses put together – Orwell manages to introduce a degree of vulnerability into his character when he describes Boxer, stating that having a 'white stripe down his nose gave him a somewhat stupid appearance'. The fact that he is 'not of first-rate intelligence' makes him an easy target for manipulation and exploitation by the pigs, which increases our sympathy for him.

After the Rebellion Orwell presents Boxer as the inspiration to all the animals, especially with his motto of 'I will work harder'. He gets up earlier and works later than the other animals. Through this selfless dedication Orwell makes Boxer's callous betrayal by Napoleon all the more tragic and heart-wrenching, thus maximising his criticism of the pigs and therefore the ruling powers of Stalinist Russia, especially Stalin himself.

1 An immediate focus on answering the question and going beneath the surface layer of the text, which is important to gain the higher marks.

2 The same point as Student X but more detailed and showing awareness of the writer.

3 Beginning to explore the writer's methods.

4 Using quotations and close textual reference to support points made.

5 Maintaining focus on the author's methods of presenting his message of betrayal and the corrupting influence of power in society.

This opening is clearly at a higher level as it is beginning to consider Orwell's methods in a thoughtful and exploratory style, rather than just showing a clear understanding of the text.

Student X continues their response as follows:

1 Continued, sustained focus on Boxer.

> As well as making Boxer the most loyal of Napoleon's followers, Orwell makes his fatal collapse a result of over work for the benefit of the farm, which is in complete contrast to the luxury lifestyle of the pigs. This represents the loyal working class being exploited by their rulers. Napoleon uses the admiration the other animals have for Boxer for his own ends when he tells them that they should take Boxer's mottos for themselves. Boxer has added another motto, 'Napoleon is always right' which is his answer to every problem and every event that he can't understand. For example, after Squealer tells the animals that Snowball was in league with Jones at the Battle of the Cowshed, Boxer is hesitant to accept this until Squealer says that Napoleon has stated that this is so. Boxer then says that if 'Comrade Napoleon says it, it must be right.' This use of deceit and propaganda shows how easily Boxer, and people in general, can be manipulated and exploited.

2 Some awareness of the writer's ideas.

Student Y's response covers similar material but in greater depth and explores beyond the surface:

2 Beginning to explore alternative interpretations.

> Orwell contrasts the fatal collapse of Boxer, due to overwork, with the indulgent lifestyle of the pigs to bring out both the greed of the pigs/rulers and their exploitation of the animals/working classes, which is one of the major themes of the novel. With Boxer's new motto ('Napoleon is always right'), however, is Orwell also criticising the unquestioning obedience of people – perhaps implying that people get the rulers they deserve? This complete acceptance of what they are told allows for a rewrite of history that strengthens the position of dictators, for example

1 Continued focus on both the presentation of Boxer and the author's ideas.

Squealer's use of propaganda to brand Snowball a traitor, so legitimising Napoleon's position. At first Boxer is hesitant to accept this, until Squealer states that Napoleon has 'categorically stated' that it is so. Boxer's response ('If Comrade Napoleon says it, it must be right') is a criticism both of totalitarianism rewriting history and also of people who accept without question what they are told. Orwell highlights the cynical manipulation by Napoleon when, after Boxer's death, he tells the other animals that they would do well to accept Boxer's mottos as their own.

3 Continued focus on Orwell's methods.

Student X then writes about Boxer being taken away in Simmonds's van:

Boxer being taking to the knacker's is the most moving part of the novel as Orwell is able to manipulate the reader's feelings by his pitiful description of the animals saying good-bye to Boxer. Only Benjamin knows what is really happening but is too late to stop the van driving Boxer away to his death. Old Major said this would happen to him. The final insult is when the pigs buy a case of whisky with the proceeds of the sale to Simmonds.

1 Relevant comment but lacking explanation of *how* exactly Orwell is manipulating the reader's feelings.

Student Y's comments on the same incident:

The importance of Boxer being taken away in Simmonds's van can be gauged by the fact that it is the only event that rouses the cynical donkey, Benjamin, to action, even though he is too late to save Boxer. Orwell foreshadowed Boxer's death at the beginning of the novel in old Major's speech, when he described exactly the eventual fate of Boxer. The significance of using this device is to show the reader that there is no difference between humans and the pigs in their treatment and attitude towards the other animals. This similarity of course reaches its climax at the very end of the novel when there is literally no difference between pigs and humans. Orwell also uses irony to highlight the pathos of this event by the fond farewells the animals give to Boxer and also by reference to the white stripe down his nose that reminds us of his lack of intelligence and therefore his vulnerability. The final humiliation and betrayal of Boxer is the buying of a case of whisky from the proceeds of his sale. This sickens us and reveals the utter cynicism and callousness of the pigs; the total indifference of tyrants to their subjects.

1 A more detailed and thoughtful exploration of this important incident, which focuses on Orwell's methods and ideas rather than merely commenting on the incident.

Student X's essay ends in the following manner:

Orwell has shown Boxer to be an important character in 'Animal Farm' as he is mostly responsible for the farm succeeding after the Rebellion and also because he represents the working class in the Russian Revolution, who were betrayed and exploited by Stalin and the Communist leaders.

1 A conclusion that, like the rest of the essay, continues to explain Boxer's role in Orwell's presentation of ideas about betrayal and corruption. The response is worthy of a Grade 5 as it reveals clear understanding.

Student Y's essay ends as follows:

Boxer's fate serves as a warning both against totalitarianism and that rulers must be held to account for their actions and people must be ever-vigilant if their utopian ideals are to become a reality. However, it can also be argued that the fate of such a strong, admirable character serves not as a warning but as a pessimistic inevitability that tyrants will always triumph and subjugate their people, by whatever means necessary.

1 A strong, thoughtful conclusion, demonstrating insight into Orwell's methods and exploring some of his ideas through the character of Boxer. The response is worthy of a Grade 8.

Student Y's essay should not be regarded as a 'perfect' essay. In the time allowed in an exam it will be impossible to explore every aspect of the question. Don't worry about this – the examiner will reward what you have written and won't penalise you for what you *haven't* written!

The question below is a typical Edexcel theme-based question.

'If she [Clover] could have spoken her thoughts, it would be to say that this was not what they had aimed at when they had set themselves years ago to work for the overthrow of the human race.'

Explore the conflict between the wished-for ideal and the actual reality in *Animal Farm*.

You must refer to the context of the novel in your answer.

Student X, who is working at around Grade 5, begins their response like this:

1 Focus on the question; shows understanding of what the book is essentially about (A01).

4 Shows understanding of how the ideal world is corrupted by the pigs, but the reference again to rules rather than commandments is simplistic. (A01).

> I am going to write about how Orwell shows that 'Animal Farm' is based on an ideal which goes wrong. Old Major explains this ideal in his speech and the song that the animals sing shows this ideal. The song says 'for that day we all must labour', meaning that the animals need to work towards this ideal of animals ruling themselves. The farm is built around this ideal and the rules show this. When the pigs start to break the rules we know that the real world is starting to come into play.

2 Key symbols and incidents are noted, but not naming the song suggests that the knowledge of detail is limited. (A01, A02).

3 Again some knowledge of the text is shown but remains vague (A01).

Although this is a reasonable start to an exam essay, an even better response appears below.

Student Y is working at around Grade 8. Carefully compare the differences between the two responses.

1 Strong focus on the question with an indication of how Orwell shows the difference between ideal and real; clear reference to the book and its political basis (A01, A03).

> In 'Animal Farm', Orwell explores the difference between ideal and real through his presentation of life post-Rebellion. Life after the Rebellion is initially based on old Major's utopian ideals, but later the farm comes under Napoleon's rule and becomes a dystopian nightmare, akin to the extremes of a totalitarian government. Orwell drew much of his material

from Russian history and his own experiences in the Spanish Civil War; this is apparent in the first chapter when we see parallels between old Major and figures such as Marx and Lenin. The system that the animals create, based on old Major's speech, is named Animalism and has links with socialism in its call for equality and collective ownership. Orwell emphasises the wonder of this post-Rebellion world and presents it as idyllic when he describes the animals waking to a new 'dawn' and looking around in the 'clear morning light', implying the spiritual and pure nature of this world.

2 Clear development of the first point, demonstrating a strong understanding of the novel in context (AO3).

This opening is clearly at a higher level as it is beginning to consider Orwell's methods in a thoughtful and exploratory style, rather than just showing a clear understanding of the text.

Student X continues their response as follows:

The pigs have created the beginnings of an ideal world by making the Seven Commandments, which Snowball reduces to one maxim — 'Four legs good, two legs bad'. However, almost immediately they start to break them when Napoleon keeps the milk. Old Major had insisted that 'all animals are equal' but Napoleon clearly shows that this is not the case under his rule.

1 More specific comments and textual support (AO1).

The reality of life on the farm continues to be different from the ideal as the pigs become more corrupt and seize more power. They move into the farmhouse, sleep in beds (breaking the 4th Commandment), execute other animals (breaking the 6th Commandment), wear clothes (breaking the 3rd Commandment) and drink alcohol (breaking the 5th Commandment). Eventually they reverse the most basic principle of Animalism: 'All animals are equal' by adding 'But some animals are more equal than others.' The pigs are able to maintain control and thus destroy old Major's vision by lies and deception, mostly through Squealer, who represents the organ of

2 Good response to AO1.

propaganda in Stalinist Russia. He is able to convince the animals that Snowball was a traitor, that the Commandments have not been changed and through the use of meaningless statistics to delude the animals into thinking they are better off.

3 Some awareness of context (AO3).

Student Y's essay continues as follows:

Throughout the novel there are continual references old Major's speech to remind us of the contrast between the utopia old Major foresaw and the dystopia that is the reality of life on the farm. For example, after the horror of the mass executions the animals gather at the little knoll and Orwell tells us that these scenes they have just witnessed were not what they expected when old Major first 'stirred them to rebellion'.

1 Well embedded supporting textual detail (AO1).

The song 'Beasts of England' is also mentioned several times in the novel. It is a 'national anthem' for the animals and Orwell gives us many positive words and phrases: 'joyful tidings', 'golden future time' and 'toil for freedom's sake'. It is a constant reminder of the ideals of the revolution but also of how far short the reality has become. The reader is thus constantly made aware of the way in which the ideals are being corrupted by those in power. Even when the song is banned and replaced by an ironic one composed by Minimus (does his name suggest a minimum of talent?), the poet pig, it is still 'hummed secretly'. Perhaps Orwell is hinting that a utopian society is still a possibility? Or perhaps he is showing us the way the masses are still being deluded into believing in the ideal while being exploited by those in power who have corrupted that ideal beyond recognition. The very end of the novel suggests, in my opinion, the latter interpretation.

Orwell also presents the conflict between the utopian ideal and the dystopian reality through the structure of the novel. The distinctive circular structure of the novel is exemplified by the change of name back to

Manor Farm at the end of the novel and the fact that the other animals can't see the difference between pig and man: 'it was impossible to say which was which'. The life of the animals on the farm has reverted back to what it was at the beginning — subjugated and downtrodden. Utopia has failed; dystopia rules.

Orwell has said the taking of the milk and apples is the turning point of the novel. I think he means that this act signifies the end of the utopian dream, almost before it has started; the battle for utopia has already been lost. Similarly, the author seems to be implying that the ideals of the Russian Revolution were also doomed to failure from the start and that this is true of every revolution.

The mass executions, a representation of the 'Great Terror' and Stalin's Purges, is the clearest example that the ideals of old Major have been corrupted. This dystopian world is clearly evoked and the 'freedom' they have is conveyed through the words 'had to'. The word 'comrades' reminds the reader of the utopian ideals of the Rebellion.

2 Continued focus on the question, well supported with embedded textual references (AO1).

3 Personal interpretation firmly grounded in context (AO1, AO3).

4 A clear reference to context, supported by specific language reference (AO3).

Student X ends their essay as follows:

When Chapter 10 begins, many years have passed and the pigs seem to have complete domination over the other animals and the ideals first said by old Major are lost forever as most of the animals who took part in the Rebellion, like Snowball and Boxer, are dead and forgotten.

In conclusion, I can say that Orwell has shown the conflict between idealism and reality very well and that the reality of life on the farm is very different to the ideal the animals thought would happen and life has become worse, not better.

1 A missed opportunity to weave in some detail on more generalised context here.

2 A rather weak conclusion, adding little to the response.

Student Y's essay ends as follows:

> In my view, the final chapter, taking place many years later, demonstrates a pessimistic attitude to human nature, as Orwell shows that the pigs' corruption and power is now complete. Most of the animals who took part in the Rebellion are dead and forgotten, only Benjamin remembers but, as always, remains quiet. Victory for dystopia over utopia is now complete: some animals ARE more equal than others (and always will be)!

1 A succinct conclusion, referring back to the question and covering AO1 (with a glance at AO3 in the last four words).

Student Y's essay should not be regarded as a 'perfect' essay. In the time allowed in an exam it will be impossible to explore every aspect of the question. Don't worry about this – the examiner will reward what you have written and won't penalise you for what you *haven't* written!

Top ten

As your examination is 'closed book' you might find it helpful to memorise some quotations to use in support of your points in the examination response. If you are unsure which exam board will be setting your question, check page 73 in the 'Tackling the exams' section.

Top ten characterisation quotations

Napoleon

1 'a reputation for getting his own way'
- The first description of Napoleon; how true this becomes!

2 'the pigs liked to invent for him such names as Father of All Animals, Terror of Mankind ... Ducklings' Friend'
- Grandiose titles like these reveal the tyrant/dictator in Napoleon.

3 'When he did appear he was attended ... by a black cockerel who marched in front of him and acted as a kind of trumpeter'
- Napoleon taking on all the pomp and grandeur of a dictator.

4 'It did not seem strange when Napoleon was seen strolling in the farmhouse garden with a pipe in his mouth.'
- The physical transformation from animal to human-lookalike is nearly complete.

Snowball

5 Compared to Napoleon: 'quicker in speech ... not the same depth of character'
- This initial description of Snowball indicates his powers as an orator and contrasts him with Napoleon, hinting at the conflict to come between the two.

6 'As though Snowball were some kind of invisible influence ... menacing them with all kinds of dangers.'
- How propaganda has altered the other animals' opinion of Snowball.

Squealer

'Squealer spoke so persuasively ... that they accepted his explanation'

7

- This quotation shows Squealer's powers of persuasion as the mouthpiece of Napoleon and the organ of propaganda.

'Squealer's demeanour suddenly changed ... his little eyes darted suspicious glances from side to side.'

8

- Squealer's nasty, dangerous side is revealed here.

Boxer

'An enormous beast [with a] somewhat stupid appearance'
'the entire work of the farm seemed to rest upon his mighty shoulders'

9

- As well as describing his physical appearance, these quotations show the high regard in which Boxer is held and also the huge debt the farm owes him – without him the farm could never have succeeded.

Old Major

'All men are enemies. All animals are comrades.'

10

- Old Major's speech, summarising his key ideas.

Top ten moments in *Animal Farm*

From the song 'Beasts of England': 'Of the golden future time.'

1

- Summing up the hopes of the animals.

Moses: 'In Sugarcandy Mountain it was Sunday seven days a week'

2

- A representation of the established Church's attitude.

'They woke at dawn ... suddenly remembering the glorious thing that had happened ... raced on to the pasture together.'

3

- Suggests a new beginning, a new 'dawn' of utopia.

4 '"Never mind the milk, comrades!" cried Napoleon.'
- The turning point of the novel.

5 'The most terrifying spectacle was of Boxer, rearing up on his hind legs and striking out ... like a stallion.'
- Boxer's contribution to the Battle of the Cowshed.

6 'the whole farm was deeply divided on the subject of the windmill'
- The main source of conflict between Snowball and Napoleon, leading to Snowball's expulsion.

7 'It was not for this that she [Clover] and all the other animals had hoped and toiled.'
- Unspoken thoughts after the mass executions.

8 '"To celebrate our victory!" cried Squealer.
"What victory?" said Boxer.'
- Even Boxer questions Squealer's propaganda after the Battle of the Windmill.

9 'Luxuries of which Snowball had once taught the animals to dream ... were no longer talked about.'
- Years later and the animals' lives have not improved.

10 'Already it was impossible to say which was which.'
- The final comment by Orwell: complete destruction of the ideals of Animalism; man and pig indistinguishable.

Top ten thematic quotations

Animalism

1 'Four legs good, two legs bad'

2 'Four legs good, two legs *better*!'

'All animals are equal but some animals are more equal than others'

3

- These quotations show how the ideals of Animalism are gradually corrupted until the original ideal is completely reversed.

Hopes of utopia

'Yes it was theirs – everything they could see was theirs'

4

- The euphoria and belief that the ideal society is beginning to be achieved.

'None of the old dreams had been abandoned. The Republic of the Animals, which Major had foretold ... was still believed in.'

5

'and yet the animals never gave up hope ... they were still the only farm owned and operated by animals.'

6

- Two quotations showing that despite all that has happened to them, the animals still believe they will achieve the perfect society.

Greed and corruption

'the farm had grown richer without making the animals themselves any richer except ... for the pigs and the dogs.'

7

- Evidence of the corruption and greed in the novel.

'it was agreed ... the milk and windfall apples should be reserved for the pigs alone.'

8

- The beginning of the pigs' manipulation of the animals for their own ends.

Abuse of power

'there was a pile of corpses lying before Napoleon's feet.'

9

- Evidence of Napoleon's reign of terror and destruction of the animals' dreams.

'he [Napoleon] carried a whip in his trotter.'

10

- The whip is a symbol of Man's oppression – the pigs are becoming more human than animal.

Wider reading

George Orwell's other novels

- *Burmese Days* (1934)
- *A Clergyman's Daughter* (1935)
- *Keep the Aspidistra Flying* (1936)
- *Coming Up for Air* (1939)
- *Nineteen Eighty-Four* (1949)

Some of Orwell's non-fiction writings especially relevant to *Animal Farm*

- *Down and Out in Paris and London* (1933)
- *The Road to Wigan Pier* (1937)
- *Homage to Catalonia* (1938)

Novels covering the period or themes explored in *Animal Farm*

- Koestler, A. *Darkness at Noon* – a novel set in 1938 during Stalin's Great Purge and show trials.
- Atwood, M. *The Handmaid's Tale* – a dystopian novel set in a dictatorship in the near future, exploring the subjugation of women.
- Huxley, A. *Brave New World* – described as a 'negative utopia' by the author, it is set in a highly scientific world in the future.
- Bradbury, R. *Fahrenheit 451* – a dystopian novel set in a USA where books are banned and 'firemen' burn any books they find (the title refers to the burning point of paper).
- Dashner, J. *The Maze Runner* – the first book in a post-apocalyptic dystopian science fiction trilogy.
- Solzhenitsyn, A. *One Day in the Life of Ivan Denisovich* – a novel set in a Soviet labour camp, which describes a single day of an ordinary prisoner who, though innocent, has been sentenced to 10 years' hard labour.

Useful websites

- www.george-orwell.org – a website dedicated to George Orwell.
- www.goodreads.com/author/show/3706.George_Orwell – contains information on Orwell's life and works, with several useful links to other websites about George Orwell and his works.
- www.online-literature.com/orwell – contains a quite detailed biography of George Orwell and also forum posts and quizzes.

- www.k-1.com/Orwell – a website dedicated to the life and work of George Orwell.
- www.resort.com/~prime8/Orwell – a brief introduction to George Orwell and links to his political writings.

Critical works on George Orwell and *Animal Farm*

- Rai, A. *Orwell and the Politics of Despair: A critical study of the writings of George Orwell* – https://books.google.com/books?isbn=0521397472
- A Critical Analysis of George Orwell's *Animal Farm* – www.academia.edu/6657939/_how_swnish_yet_a_crtical_analysis_of_george_orwell_s_animal_farm

Answers

Answers to the 'Review your learning' sections.

Context (p. 15)

1 Eric Blair. It may have been his way of shedding his old middle-class identity and taking on a new one.

2 He became disillusioned with socialism and realised that there is something in human nature that will always seek power over others.

3 Themes of totalitarianism and personality cult are in both novels.

4 Two examples (there are many more):
   - Tsar Nicholas II is deposed and Mr Jones is run out of Manor Farm.
   - Trotsky and Stalin battle for leadership after Lenin dies and Snowball and Napoleon battle over leadership of Animal Farm.

5 Stalin was held in high regard in England at that time and the government did not want to offend him.

Plot and structure (p. 35)

1 Manor Farm.

2 Animalism.

3 'Four legs good, two legs bad.'

4 Mr Pilkington (Foxwood Farm) and Mr Frederick (Pinchfield Farm).

5 Snowball *was* winning the debate but was then driven out of the farm so Napoleon won; but he then took over Snowball's idea!

6 The pigs move into the farmhouse and sleep in beds, but without sheets.

7 The food bins are filled with sand with only a thin layer of grain and meal on the top.

8 The pigs get drunk on whisky and Napoleon wears a hat.

9 A crate of whisky.

10 'All animals are equal but some animals are more equal than others.'

11 Its circular structure.

Characterisation (p. 48)

1
   - author's description
   - what characters say and how they say it
   - what characters think and do
   - what others say and think about them
   - what they represent.

2   Some examples for Napoleon: ruthless, cruel and hypocritical. These negative adjectives reveal Napoleon's tyrannical nature and are some of the qualities of a totalitarian ruler.
Some examples for Snowball: creative, eloquent and courageous. These positive adjectives contrast with the negative description of Napoleon and reveal Snowball's heroic nature.

3   The sheep.

4   Moses the raven.

5   ● Marx = old Major
    ● Stalin = Napoleon
    ● Trotsky = Snowball
    ● Defectors to the West = Mollie
    ● Secret Police = the dogs.

Themes (p. 62)

1   They are an expression of the writer's key ideas.

2   The Russian Revolution and its subsequent events.

3   For example: abuse of power, greed and corruption, idealism vs reality, violence, propaganda, personality cult, totalitarianism.

4   For example: propaganda, totalitarianism.

5   ● Jones fires a shotgun into the night.
    ● Minor casualties in the Battle of the Cowshed.
    ● Disagreements between Snowball and Napoleon escalate until Napoleon urinates on Snowball's plans.
    ● Snowball is chased off the farm and the death sentence given to him in his absence.
    ● The hens are starved into submission (nine hens die).
    ● Four pigs and three hens who disagreed with Napoleon are killed by his dogs.
    ● Lots of other animals are then slaughtered. The dogs also attack Boxer.
    ● Lots of casualties in the violent Battle of the Windmill.

6   'Who controls the past controls the future; who controls the present controls the past.'

Language, style and analysis (p. 71)

1   It is a story with talking animals (fable/allegory).

2   ● Writing the novel as an easily understood fable.
    ● Paralleling key events of the Russian Revolution.
    ● Pigs gradually adopting all the worst human characteristics until they are indistinguishable from humans.

3   It can emphasise a key emotion or idea by placing it at the start of the sentence.

4   The Russian Revolution and subsequent events up to 1943.

5   It helps to show that life for the animals is as bad now as it was at the beginning of the novel.

6   Where the author gives a hint to the reader of what will happen in the story.

7   For example, read the part of old Major's speech where he talks about Boxer's likely end and compare this with the actual end of Boxer.

8   Chapters 1–9 cover four years.

Tackling the exams (p. 80)

1   Yes, for AQA and Edexcel; up to 4 marks. OCR does not examine SPaG in the question on *Animal Farm*.

2   No.

3   It helps you to organise your thoughts.

4   Check your meaning is clear; check you haven't missed any important points; check your spelling, punctuation and grammar.

5   Two examples would be:
   - 'How…'
   - 'Explore…'

6   Two examples would be:
   - 'however…'
   - 'when…'

Assessment Objectives and skills (p. 85)

1   Your ability to read, understand and respond to texts.

2   Your ability to analyse the language, form and structure used by a writer.

3   Your ability to show understanding between texts and the contexts in which they were written.

4   Your spelling, punctuation and grammar.

5   If you don't know, ask your teacher. Check page 73 in the 'Tackling the exams' section for the AOs you need to focus on. (All boards assess AO1 and AO3.)

6
   - Retell the story.
   - Use long quotations.
   - Merely identify literary devices.
   - Give unsupported opinions.
   - Write about characters as if they were real people.